— WHAT OTHERS ARE SAYING —

Straight-Up Crazy is the perfect book for anyone who desires a fresh infusion of radical faith! If your Christian journey has felt safe, comfortable, "normal," or even boring, Paulette's enthusiasm and passion will have you ready to step out of the "stinkin' boat" and experience the joy of "walking on the water" in no time! Not only does Paulette do an excellent job of unpacking God's Word in a relevant and powerful way, she weaves in her own personal insecurities and victories with transparency and authenticity. Paulette writes not as a distant teacher, but as a fellow sojourner, a personal cheerleader, a trusted girlfriend reminding you who God is and what He is able to do! Before long, you'll be "craving the crazy" too! My sense is as you read *Straight-Up Crazy*, you'll create a list of others you know who would enjoy Paulette's passionate and fun teaching style. Trust me, you'll want to read it for yourself first, and then pass it along! It's that good! -Cindy Bultema, Speaker and Author of *Red Hot Faith: Lessons from a Lukewarm Church*

Have you ever stood on the precipice of an amazing adventure, yet the fear of the unknown has kept you clinging to the comfort of your "normal" lifestyle? Straight-Up Crazy is the nudge that will tip you over the edge of, "*I believe* Jesus has a plan for my life" to "*I am experiencing* His extraordinary and exciting destiny for me!" Paulette Stamper has an amazing gift that inspires the family of God to go beyond the natural and live a supernatural life that is so crazy it could only be His power that is working through the limitation of our humanity. Read this book, if you dare, and you too will hear the call to JUMP off the edge of normal Christianity. You will find yourself smack dab in the middle of a great-big-God-produced-possible that will thrill and delight you as your radical faith begins to change the world. —Amy Byrd, Speaker and Author of *Blessed Beyond Belief: Claiming Your Rights in Christ*

Paulette takes familiar stories from the Bible many of us have heard over and over, but drags us into that boat with Peter and all the other disciples. As I read chapter 4, I could see myself in the boat wondering if I live my life in safety or if I was a "water walker" with Jesus. And then I had to consider: Is "safety" really worth it? Do I desire "normal" over Jesus? And if so, for what am I settling? *Straight-Up Crazy* challenges me to fulfill what it means to follow Christ…to do life differently, even if it means I might look a little nuts in the eyes of the world. —Jennifer Ferguson, co-author of *Pure Eyes, Clean Heart: A Couple's Journey to Freedom from Pornography*

Paulette Stamper's writing is engaging, challenging, and encouraging all at once. She powerfully presents a viewpoint that as followers of Christ we should desire to walk in His footsteps, understanding that there will be moments when He will ask us, to step out of our boats. She illustrates well that when that happens we may be in over our heads and that will cause us to turn to Him all the more. —David J. Wright, Vice President of Ministry Services, TCM International Institute

STRAIGHT-UP CRAZY

a call to **radical** faith

ignite
WOMEN™

ignitewomen.com

STRAIGHT-UP CRAZY

a call to **radical** faith

Published in Indianapolis, Indiana by Ignite Women. Ignite Women is
a registered trademark or Ignite Women, Inc.

Unless otherwise noted, Scripture quotations are taken from the
Holy Bible, New International Version®, NIV®. ©1973, 1978, 1984, 2011
by Biblica, Inc.™ Used by permission by Zondervan. All rights reserved
worldwide. www.zondervan.com

Scripture quotations marked KJV are from the King James Version.
Public domain.

Scripture quotations marked MSG are from *The Message* by
Eugene H. Peterson. ©1993, 1994, 1995, 1996, 2000. Used by permission
of NavPress Publishing Group. All rights reserved.

Scripture quotations marked NKJV™ are taken from the New King
James Version®. ©1982 by Thomas Nelson, Inc. Used by permission.
All rights reserved.

Cover and book design by Dustin Brenton.

ISBN 978-0-9850114-7-5

——————— DEDICATED TO ———————

To my amazing husband, Jake. You keep me sane. You push me when I need to be pushed. You pull me when I need to be pulled. You make me laugh harder than anyone else on the planet. You make me a better person. We've been doing straight-up crazy since that first collect phone call twenty-one years ago. Let's keep it going. I am madly in love with you.

ACKNOWLEDGMENTS

Lise Caldwell, I cannot express with words my gratitude for your willingness to take on this project and your encouraging words along the way. There's NO WAY I could have done this without you! Thank you!! I adore you!

What does it say about me when I need an entire team of proof readers? Carla Abbott, Clair Beller and Danielle Hofer, you ladies are the best! Thank you for your sharp eye and your willingness to comb over this with precision – and in a time crunch at that!

The beautiful women on Ignite leadership team - Stephanie Wright, Carla Abbott, Dene Nidiffer, Peg Daly, Danielle Hofer, Kim Dollard and Sarah Brennan. Your continued support and prayers keep me going and keep me sane. Well, almost sane anyway!

Dustin Brenton, aka Super Dustin, thank you for working your magic again! Dude. You're awesome.

SPECIAL THANKS

To the special ladies who wrote the Coffee Chat and Personal Study Questions at the end of each chapter: Kim Roberts, Mel Carroll, Dene Nidiffer, Bekah Kidd, Carla Abbott, Jess Scott and Erika Scheck. You ladies are awesome!

CONTENTS

Chapter One
Destiny Change 13

Chapter Two
Big Buts 37

Chapter Three
Radical Trust and Crazy Obedience 59

Chapter Four
Craving the Crazy 81

Chapter Five
Get Your Fight On 105

Chapter Six
Crank Up the Victory Tunes 129

Chapter Seven
A New Kind of Math 151

Chapter Eight
Not Quite Finished Just Yet 177

Epilogue
Run the Race • Fight the Good Fight • Get the Prize 201

CHAPTER ONE
DESTINY CHANGE

Without faith it is impossible to please God, because anyone who comes to Him must believe that He exists and that He rewards those who earnestly seek Him. Hebrews 11:6

"Want God to do something new in your life? Stop doing the same thing! Endings are the perfect place for a new start." Christine Caine[1]

"What's so beautiful about our call is that God knows full well whom He's getting when He calls us." Susie Larson[2]

What would it take to change your destiny? Winning the lottery? Inheriting a fortune? Landing a dream job in a dream career? Marrying a soul-mate?

I can't help but wonder what you thought when you read the title of this chapter. Maybe when you thought about a change in destiny, you thought about what your life would look like if you changed careers. Or maybe how your life would be different if you moved to a different city. Or maybe you imagine every now and then what it would be like to not be stuck in a rut. To believe that what you do from day to day actually mattered on a grander scale. We all want to matter. It's a basic human desire to want to be a part of something outside of ourselves that brings meaning to life. We are all born with an inner desire for significance and worth. We all believe we were born to have an extraordinary destiny. Well, we want to believe that, but do we really believe it?

WHAT IF?

Let's play the "What if?" game for a minute. What if your destiny has eternal significance? What if you weren't meant to play it safe your entire life? What if there is more to life than getting married and having 2.5 kids and a great career, and buying a nice house in the suburbs (with a white picket fence and if you're lucky, a pool)? What if you were meant to experience God doing impossible things, both in you and through you? What if 'extraordinary' was the word you regularly used to describe God's activity in your life? Think that all sounds a bit ridiculous? Far-fetched? Actually, it's not far-fetched at all. I'm convinced that extraordinary should be your ordinary. And it all begins with a destiny change.

Consider Moses. Circumstances weren't exactly stacked in his favor when he was born. His mom did what she had to do to save him from Pharaoh's death mandate. Next thing she knew her son was being raised by Pharaoh's daughter. She would have never imagined that his life would turn out the way it did. She would have had no reason to suspect that her son's future resume would include both Murderer and Rescuer. One of my favorite things about God is the way He delights in doing the unexpected.

We're going to be spending a lot of time with Moses, so I encourage you to set this book down and pick up your Bible and read Exodus 1-3 as a refresher. No really. Do it.

Moses. I honestly think I could study Moses for the rest of my life and never grow tired or bored with him. It's no secret to anyone who knows me, Exodus 3 is my favorite passage of Scripture in the entire Bible. I believe that God reveals Himself so clearly in this passage and reveals more about Himself than He ever had since Creation. This amazing encounter was a clear turning point for Moses. His entire destiny changed that day at the burning bush. He thought his life was going in one direction and God completely turned it around.

There's no way Moses could have known that on that particular day his entire life was about to get straight-up crazy. (And I mean the good kind of crazy, the crazy that only God can orchestrate. Not the bad kind of crazy, like "you-shouldn't-have-worn-that-tubetop-to-Wal-Mart-crazy"[1]). Crazy was his destiny. I happen to believe that crazy is the destiny God wants for all of us who follow Him.

Let's face it. Moses probably believed he'd blown it with the whole murder thing, so he ran off to the desert and settled there. I have watched this happen over and over again in the lives of some people I know. They flee to the desert to hide from their past. Without even thinking about it, they settle in and make the desert their home. It's not like Moses planned on murdering an Egyptian, but before he knew it, he was burying a dude in the sand and running as fast as he could toward the desert. He ended up far from what he thought his life would be. Instead of living a life of royalty and luxury in Egypt, he found himself with a staff in his hand herding sheep. Not exactly the career and location he would have chosen. Sound familiar? Maybe you can relate to Moses. Have you ever wondered, "How did I end up here? Why did my life turn out this way?" Pretty sure Moses would have asked himself the same questions repeatedly. Nevertheless, there he was, living in the desert herding sheep. Until…

[1]Thank you for this quote, Laura Dingman. It cracks me up every time!

*The angel of the Lord appeared to him in flames of fire
from within a bush. Exodus 3:2*

Don't you love that God initiated the encounter? He always does. This encounter changed everything for Moses. It was the beginning of a holy, radical, straight-up crazy destiny change.

You know those dudes that chase storms? They constantly monitor the weather conditions and deliberately run toward the path of severe storms hoping for a glimpse of a tornado. I think those guys are crazy. And not the good kind of crazy. Moses wasn't like that. He wasn't a burning bush chaser. He didn't wake up that particular morning and think the conditions in the air were ripe for a burning bush and his destiny change was on the horizon. He woke up that morning like any other morning, grabbed his staff, kissed the wife and kiddos good-bye and headed to the office. What started out as a normal day turned into the most non-normal day he'd ever had. (At least up until that point anyway!) This particular day, something caught his attention out of the corner of his eye. He saw the strangest sight – a bush on fire but it wasn't being consumed. He couldn't help but wonder about it so he goes to investigate. Exodus 3:4 tells us that "the Lord saw that [Moses] had gone over to look." The meaning of this phrase in the Hebrew is worth mentioning. It paints a picture of God leaning over and watching

Moses carefully to see how he would respond to the burning bush. God planned out this scene, set it up, then watched closely, waiting to see how Moses would respond. God's next move would be based on Moses' response. It was only when Moses went over to the bush that God spoke, calling him by name. (I can't help but wonder, did the angels applaud in excitement when they saw Moses approach the burning bush? Did they lean in to hear the ensuing conversation?) When Moses reached the bush, immediately God told him to remove his sandals because the place where he was standing was holy ground. Why was that particular section of dirt holy? Because God transforms the ordinary into holy merely by His presence. God identified Himself as the God of Abraham, Isaac and Jacob. Based on Moses' reaction, he was familiar with the stories of his ancestors, because he hid his face in fear. A healthy fear, indeed.

—A GOD WHO REVEALS HIMSELF—

Moses' destiny change began the moment God revealed Himself. And just how did God reveal Himself? As the God who sees, hears, knows and comes down to rescue. "I have seen the misery of my people in Egypt," God says in Exodus 3:7. God witnessed all of the persecution, injustice and sorrow that had been inflicted on the Israelites by the Egyptians. Not a moment of their suffering had escaped His sight. The Lord goes on to say, "I have heard them crying out because of their slave masters." The cries of their pain and anguish had reached His ears. The heart of God is moved by sincere prayers for help and rescue. He continues, "I am concerned about their suffering." The KJV renders this verse "for I know their sorrows." The word "know" is the Hebrew word "yada" and it means "to perceive and see, to distinguish, to be acquainted with, to have knowledge, to know by experience."[1] Let that definition sink in for a minute. God understood and perceived, at the most intimate level, the suffering of His children. He wasn't casually observing the misery and distress from His throne in heaven, unmoved or unaffected. Rather, He was intimately moved by their sorrow and pain. He concludes, "So I have come down to rescue them from the hand of the Egyptians." The phrase "come down" in the Hebrew means, "to go down, descend, to come down."[2] The meaning of this phrase is very literal. God is declaring that He Himself has come down to rescue His children from a force greater than themselves. They did not possess the ability or power to free themselves from the bondage of the Egyptians. These four statements clearly reveal the heart and motive of God toward His children; He sees their misery, He hears their cries, and He knows their sorrows, so He comes down to rescue them. What an awesome revelation of the God of the uni-

[1] Strong's Exhaustive Concordance
[2] Ibid

He was and is and will forever be a God who sees, hears, knows and **rescues**!

verse! He was and is and will forever be a God who sees, hears, knows and rescues! This incredible revelation was the beginning of Moses' radical destiny change.

Like Moses, our destiny change always comes in two parts. A revelation of God followed by a call to respond. The revelation is God's part. He reveals Himself to us. The response part is up to us. There is never a revelation without a call to respond.

—————— SO NOW, GO ——————

Immediately after the revelation in Exodus 3, God said to Moses, "So now, go. I am sending you to Pharaoh to bring My people the Israelites out of Egypt." We will deal with Moses' less than ideal initial response to his calling in the next chapter. But for now, focus on the incredible significance of what had just happened. This encounter changed Moses' life and ultimately changed the entire life trajectory of millions more. Dude. This encounter was massively significant. Moses thought his destiny consisted of being a shepherd of sheep, but

God said, "Your destiny is to shepherd my people." Moses thought his destiny was to wander in the desert, but God said, "Your destiny is to lead my people through the desert and to the Promised Land." Moses thought his destiny was to live the rest of his life hiding because of what he had done in the past. But God said, "I see you Moses. I know all about you and all you have done. I will rescue you, Moses. No more hiding in the desert. I have plans for you. I am calling you to go rescue others. This is your straight-up crazy destiny."[1] Moses went on to lead the entire nation of Israel out of bondage and captivity and to the Promised Land. And it all began with a revelation and a call to respond.

Granted, it's easy to read this account in Scripture and point to this encounter as Moses' destiny change. It's easy to see the revelation of God and the call to respond. I bet some of you are already thinking, "I love this story, but I'm interested in knowing how *my* destiny can change. I've never had a burning bush in my backyard. I have never heard God speak audibly. My life pretty much looks the same as it always has. Nothing radical going on over here. No encounters that could be described as supernatural or extraordinary. I'm still waiting and hoping God will reveal Himself to me like He did to Moses." If that's what you are thinking then I hope to change your thinking by the

[1] Obviously these are not direct quotes.

> **God** does the calling – **you** do the responding.

end of this chapter. Ready? Here we go. I'll just come straight out of the gate with it: If you are a believer in Jesus Christ and have surrendered your life to Him as your Lord and Savior, then your destiny has already been radically changed.

Your salvation experience was your burning bush experience.

Think that sounds crazy? Then let me give you a few points to consider. God initiated the encounter with Moses, not the other way around. It was the same for you. You did not initiate your first encounter with God. He sought you out first. You love God because He first loved you (1 John 4:19). He does the calling - you do the responding. God revealed Himself to Moses as the God who sees, hears, knows and rescues. He is the same God yesterday, today and forever (Hebrews 13:8). The God that saw the Israelites and heard them crying out is the same God who saw you in your lost, helpless state and He heard your cries. The God who was intimately acquainted with the suffering of His children in Egypt is the same God who was acutely aware of your suffering due to sin. The God who came down to rescue the Israelites from an enemy that was too powerful for them is the same God who took on human flesh, came down to the earth He created and rescued you from the powerful enemy of your soul and out of the dominion of darkness. He rescued you by paying the ransom for your sin through Christ's death on the cross. The burning bush was Moses' radical turning point. Your confession of faith in Jesus as your Lord and Savior was your radical turning point.

Consider these "before and after" descriptions regarding your spiritual burning bush encounter. I think it will be helpful to see just a few:

> Offer yourselves to God as those who have been brought from **death** to **life**. Romans 6:13b (Emphasis mine.)

> But because of His great love for us, God, who is rich in mercy, made us **alive** with Christ even when we were **dead** in transgressions. Ephesians 2:4-5 (Emphasis mine.)

> But you are a chosen people, a royal priesthood, a holy nation, God's special possession, that you may declare the praises of Him who called you out of **darkness** and into His wonderful **light**. 1 Peter 2:9 (Emphasis mine.)

> When you were **dead** in your sins and in the uncircumcision of your flesh, God made you **alive** with Christ. Colossians 2:13 (Emphasis mine.)

──────── A RADICAL CALL ────────

The message God delivered to Moses from the burning bush is the same message that God delivered through Jesus on the cross. He sees. He hears. He knows. He rescues. You are probably like me and need to be reminded of these incredible truths on a regular basis. I fear all too often believers in Christ are waiting and hoping for a radical burning bush experience and a direct call from God into an awesome and exciting destiny. *Actually, we've already had a burning bush experience. We've already heard the call.* We've already been given a direct call from God into an awesome and breathtaking destiny. It doesn't get any more dramatic than being rescued from the dominion of darkness and brought into the kingdom of light. It doesn't get any more drastic or extreme than your destiny being radically changed from death to life. FROM DEATH TO LIFE. This begs the question, "Why do we downplay or minimize our salvation experience?" I have heard well-meaning Christians say things like, "I don't really have a testimony." What they mean is they don't have a story that tickles the ears with details like, "I was once a crack-addict/prostitute/hater of Christians/mass murderer." But what they are really saying is, "I wasn't that bad to begin with so it didn't take that much to save me." What?! That is messed up! Try to imagine how it would have sounded to the ears of God to hear Moses tell someone, "I don't really have a testimony. I mean, God revealed Himself to me when I was 83 by speaking to me from a burning bush and then told me to go rescue the Hebrews from slavery. But, well, you know, I'm still just waiting for my purpose and calling." How ridiculous is that? That mindset is incredibly insulting to God. We need to look at our salvation experience with a fresh pair of eyes so we will see just how incredible it really is. We need a fresh reminder that it took the literal death of Jesus on a wooden cross to rescue us. There is nothing ordinary or mundane about that! God is looking for men and women who will live in a constant state of awareness of exactly what it took to rescue them from darkness to light, and from death to life. It's the men and women who will humbly and gratefully embrace the significance of their salvation that God will infuse with the radical, straight-up crazy faith necessary to step into their calling and destiny.

Remember, a destiny change does not consist solely of a revelation from God - a call to respond follows. The Lord said to Moses, "So now, go. I am sending you to Pharaoh to bring my people the Israelites out of Egypt," (Exodus 3:10). Think about this. God could have spoken to Moses and revealed Himself as the God who sees, hears, knows and rescues. Moses could have said, "I believe!" then turned around, put his sandals back on, grabbed his staff and headed home, calling it a day. But that's not where it ended. God's revelation was followed by a call to respond. It always is. One of the most mind-boggling things about Almighty God who created the universe with a spoken word is that He chooses to involve us in His divine rescue plan. He could have easily brought the Israelites out of Egypt with zero participation from Moses, but that's not how God chooses to work. He initiates an encounter, reveals Himself, and then calls us to respond by participating in His divine plan.

— RESCUED FOR A REASON —

Moses was meant for more than a destiny in the desert. God radically changed his destiny by setting his life on a profoundly different course with an unparalleled calling to rescue the children of Israel. *You were meant for more than the desert.* God revealed Himself to you and radically changed your destiny. Your destiny change comes with a responsibility that has far-reaching implications. You are meant to do big things for God's kingdom. You are meant to experience Him do amazing things *in* you and *through* you. You were not put on the earth to take up oxygen and wander around searching for your life's meaning. God has an astounding purpose and plan for you as His child.

Your purpose and your destiny are rooted in God's calling on your life. Your calling is the same calling as Moses'. "**Go**. I am sending you." (Sound familiar? Matthew 28:19-20 ring any bells?)

> *Therefore go and make disciples of all nations, baptizing them in the name of the Father and of the Son and of the Holy Spirit, and teaching them to obey everything I have commanded you. And surely I am with you always, to the very end of the age.*

I can't think of a better, clearer explanation of your calling, in Scripture, than this passage in 2 Corinthians 5:17-21:

> *Therefore, if anyone is in Christ, he is a new creation; the old has gone, the new has come! All this is from God, who reconciled us to Himself through Christ and **gave us the ministry of reconciliation**: that God was reconciling the world to Himself in Christ, not counting people's sins against them. **And He has committed to us the message of reconciliation.** We are therefore Christ's ambassadors, as though God were making His appeal through us. We implore you on Christ's behalf: Be reconciled to God. God made Him who had no sin to be sin for us, so that in Him we might become the righteousness of God.* (Emphasis mine.)

You are a new creation in Christ. Rescued from the dominion of darkness and brought into light. Rescued from death to life. God has given you the same call He gave Moses. "Go." He rescued the Israelites *through* Moses. He will rescue those around you *through* you. You are called to make known the God who sees, hears, knows, and rescues. No more waiting around and hoping God calls you. *He already has.* No more dreaming about a radical destiny. *You've already been given one.* No more just hoping God will do amazing things through you. *He's already begun by doing amazing things IN you.* You have been given the highest calling and most radical destiny that exists:

You were rescued so you can go rescue.

While every follower of Christ has the same calling, our destinies are unique to each of us. Paul writes in Ephesians 2:10, "We are God's handiwork, created in Christ Jesus to do good works, which God prepared in advance for us to do." Your calling is to go rescue. Your destiny lies in the good works that He has prepared for you. He will equip you and empower you to accomplish amazing things that He has planned just for you. Imagine that. God planned and mapped out your destiny before He spoke the universe into existence. Your destiny won't be ordinary. Or mundane. Or boring. Or meaningless. Or easy. Or something you can do on your own, in your own strength and knowledge. It will require faith. Crazy faith. And determination. And perseverance. And belief. And trust. And it will include unspeakable joy and amazement along the way. It will result in an intimacy with your Savior and Redeemer that you could have never imagined.

I hope I've managed to convince you that your destiny was radically changed at your salvation. However, there are always some believers who are convinced that they've blown it and there's no way God would call them to do anything, let alone something crazy and radical. If that describes you, then let me ask you to con- sider Moses again. I bet he thought he'd blown it, too. I mean, he did kill a dude and all, and then ran and hid in the desert. He did the same thing

> While **every follower** of Christ has the same calling, our destinies are **unique** to each of us.

day in and day out for 40 long years. He had been there for so long, he probably had a nice retirement saved up and was ready to live out the rest of his life on a beach somewhere with the Mrs., but God had other plans. There were good works that God had prepared for Moses to do *before* creation. Even murdering the Egyptian couldn't thwart

God's destiny for Moses. Maybe you've been hiding from something you did in your past for so long that you believe there's no chance that God could still have a plan for your life. Let's see. How can I put this delicately? Um, you're wrong! If you are still breathing then you can still step into your God given destiny. Moses was 83 when he stepped into his crazy destiny. Are you 83? Probably not. Then it's time for you to get your move on. (If you are 83, will you call me? I want to hear your story!)

Let's play another round of the "What if?" game. What if you made the decision today to think about your salvation experience as your destiny change? What if you embraced the truth that God set your life on a different course the day you professed your belief in Christ? What if you chose to believe that the God that called Moses to "go" is the same God that has called you to "go"? Your first step in the direction of having straight-up crazy faith, breaking free from the ordinary and mundane, finding meaning and divine purpose in your life, is to embrace the truth of your destiny change. Open your eyes. Embrace your calling, and better yet, embrace the God who has called you, and choose to believe that He will use you to do some crazy big things.

If you have come to the end of this chapter and realized you have never had a personal salvation "burning bush" experience and would like to, why not today? Why not right now? Simply pray and admit to God your need for a Savior. Confess your sin and ask for forgiveness. Believe in the Lord Jesus Christ then take the first step of obedience and get baptized. And make sure you tell someone!

—PERSONAL STUDY QUESTIONS—

1. Carefully read the following Scriptures: Jeremiah 29:11, Romans 8:28 and Psalm 139:1-18. Consider the following questions:

   a. What do these truths in God's Word show you about God's role in your destiny?

   b. How does believing these truths change how you perceive your destiny?

   c. When you consider God's plans for your life include prospering you, giving you hope and a future, what does that reveal to you about His heart toward you? In what ways can you demonstrate with your words and actions your gratitude to God?

   d. How are you trusting God to work the circumstances in your life for good? Do you personally feel called "according to His purpose"?

   e. How does knowing that the God of the universe is intimately involved in every detail of your life change your perspective regarding your destiny?

f. Consider starting a "life journal" and write in detail about the moments and experiences that helped shape who you are. Prayerfully examine each major experience and be willing to ask God to use it for good.

g. What do you remember about your salvation experience? Have you ever thought about it as a "burning bush" experience like Moses had? Take some time to think about the events and circumstances that led to your salvation. Write a prayer to God thanking Him for initiating the encounter that changed your destiny.

2. After God revealed Himself to Moses, He then called Moses to act. In the same way, God is calling you to act. Read and reflect on James 1:22-25 and James 2:14-26. In what ways has God revealed Himself to you and in what capacity is He calling you to respond?

3. Read Exodus 3:7-8. This is the same God that you serve today. Knowing that your Heavenly Father knows what you are going through, hears your cries, is concerned with your suffering and wants to rescue you, can be very reassuring in times of trials. Write a prayer to God thanking Him for times where you have seen Him during difficult seasons in your life. Write a prayer

asking Him to help you remember in your trial that He hears you, feels your pain and wants to rescue you.

4. Read Judges 6 and answer the following questions:

   a. How is Gideon's story similar to Moses' story? In what ways is it different?

   b. Consider how Moses and Gideon both felt incapable of doing what God had called them to do. Can you relate? How have you experienced God's faithfulness during the times when you felt most powerless?

   c. God told both men "I will be with you." Consider the Scripture "I the Lord do not change" (Malachi 3:6). Write a prayer to God thanking Him that He is with you just as He was with Moses and Gideon.

5. Read Colossians 1:13-14. How can understanding that your salvation was a divine encounter and rescue change the way you respond to God's calling on your life to "go"?

COFFEE CHATS

1. Share an event in your life that helped to shape your destiny.

2. Do you live your life waiting for something or someone to come along and change the direction of your life? Or, are you actively doing things that impact the direction of your life? Explain.

3. Do you willingly share your spiritual testimony with others? Why or why not?

4. What role does God have in your day to day life?

5. Have you ever viewed your salvation as a "burning bush/destiny change" experience? Describe how viewing it this way could affect the way you talk about it with others.

Questions by Kim Roberts

CHAPTER TWO
Big bUTs

Let us run with perseverance the race marked out for us, fixing our eyes on Jesus, the pioneer and perfecter of faith. Hebrews 12:1b-2a

Since, then, you have been raised with Christ, set your hearts on things above, where Christ is, seated at the right hand of God. Set your minds on things above, not on earthly things. Colossians 3:1-2

"You can't have a right view of yourself unless you have a right view of God – that's what anchors your soul." James MacDonald[1]

FIRE IT UP!

I get fired up when I imagine countless believers across the globe convinced of their radical destiny change. Imagine what God could and would do if all of His followers were convinced that their destiny was rooted in the good works that He had planned just for them before He created the world. What if every single one of us who professed Christ as our Savior truly understood that our radical destiny is rooted in our calling to go? What would our world begin to look like if we were convinced God would do the impossible in us and through us? The hungry would be fed, the homeless would have homes, the orphans would have families, the depressed would have joy, the slaves would be set free and the fearful would become fearless, and I believe that's just for starters! I'm asking and believing God to light a fire under your tail and ignite in you an insatiable craving for a movement of the Holy Spirit in your life. I'm believing God to anoint you with a holy anticipation and desperation for His presence and power resulting in a faith that's straight-up crazy! However, I know from experience that there are obstacles we have to deal with head-on in order for us to live out a straight-up crazy faith and step boldly into our destiny and calling. These obstacles are our *big buts*. Let's face it. We've got some mighty big buts.

——————— YEAH, BUT... ———————

I have a confession. I sometimes reign as the Queen of Buts. I'm embarrassed to admit that I honestly can't think of a time when God called me to do something and I didn't respond by saying, "But God," followed by a long list of excuses as to why I was not the right person for the job. This happened to me just recently. Just when I wanted to believe that I was far too spiritually mature to tout, "But God," He asked me to do something that was not on my radar, has never been on my radar, and for that matter, I never wanted to be on my radar, neither now nor in the future. I had zero desire to do what He was calling me to do. And not only did I not want to do it, I was thoroughly convinced that I couldn't do it. I had absolutely no experience to draw from, I am not naturally gifted in this area, and I didn't have a clue how to even begin. I still hate to admit it, but if I'm being very honest, what it boiled down to was that I didn't really believe God could pull this one off. Ironically, I didn't doubt that God was calling me to do it, I just flat didn't believe I could do it. And what's worse, I didn't believe He could/would be able to do it through me. I had myself convinced that God got this one all wrong and He should have asked someone else to do it.[1] Good grief. I so know better. But I'd bet, if you were being honest, you'd admit you've wrestled with your big but too. If you are truly wanting to kick up your faith to the straight-up crazy notch then you are going to have to deal with your buts. There's no room for big buts on the crazy faith train. It's time to lay those buts on the altar. God doesn't like big buts and I cannot lie. Okay, you get the point.

[1]Wondering what it was that God called me to do? You're holding it in your hands. Pretty ironic, huh? God called me to write a book on radical faith and I didn't even have enough faith to believe He could do it. Now that's crazy. And not the good kind of crazy. I am a great example of the amazing patience and relentless pursuit of God.

So why do we pull out the big buts when God calls us to do something? Simply put, we take our eyes off of God. And why do we take our eyes off of God? Unbelief. When God knit you together in your mother's womb, He wired your brain with the ability and need to be focused on Him. When you consciously or subconsciously take your focus off of God, by default, your focus will be on something or someone else. Where you place your focus has everything to do with whether or not you will have a big but problem. If your focus is not on God, you will struggle with buts of fear, doubt and/or pride. If your focus isn't right, then when God calls you to do something, your but of fear will say, "I can't do this." Doubt will say, "God can't do this." And pride will say, "I can do this on my own without God." The root of fear, doubt and pride is unbelief and unbelief leads to a big 'ol but problem. I'm going to use my favorite Old Testament account in Exodus again to illustrate our but problem. (If you skipped reading this passage in the first chapter, now would be a good time to catch up! And go ahead and read chapter 4 while you're there.)

Immediately after God revealed Himself to Moses in the burning bush, completely changing his destiny, God issued Moses the call to go. Remember, God never reveals Himself without including a call to respond. The call always follows the revelation. Your destiny is rooted in your call. You cannot accomplish your call apart from God. Your call can never be done in your own strength or ability. God is all about the journey with you. He is all about the relationship with you. He is all about culti-vating in you an unparalleled

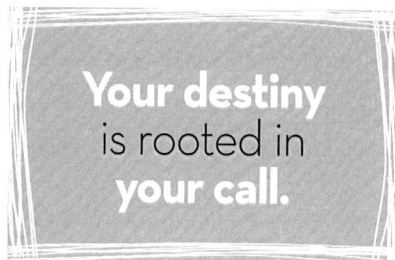

Your destiny is rooted in your call.

faith that will allow Him to do the impossible in you and through you. God will never reveal Himself to you, call you and then leave you to accomplish anything in your own strength. There's no way Moses could have done what God was calling him to do. And that is precisely the point. Moses' call required faith. Straight-up crazy, radical faith. Moses' initial response to his calling was less than ideal, yet probably very similar to what yours and mine would have been. God said, "Hey Moses, now that you know who I am, I want you to do something for me. Go back to Egypt, confront Pharaoh, and bring my people out of slavery." I hear Moses in my head saying, "Do what?!" and then it only took about 2.2 seconds (my estimate) for Moses' big but to show up.

WHO AM I?

In all fairness, Moses' initial question, "Who am I?" is an overall fan-tastic question and quite frankly, it was a very wise question for Moses to ask. Think about it. If he had puffed up his chest and immediately

declared, "I've got this! Pharaoh won't know what hit him!" then some-

thing would have been amiss. That kind of attitude would point to a

very prideful and elevated view of self. Instead, the question, "Who

am I that I should go to Pharaoh and bring the Israelites out of Egypt?"

displayed a legitimate and realistic question rooted in humility and

> But **Moses said** to God...Who am I? ... What if they don't believe me or listen to me? ... **I can't speak well!**

self-awareness of ability. He must have been thinking about how it would be dangerous for him to return. After all, he was a fugitive on the run for a very serious crime. He also would have wondered why in the world the king of Egypt would

give him the time of day. And surely he must have questioned how he

could lead well over a million people anywhere, let alone through the

desert and to the Promised Land. It's actually a good thing to ask the

question, "Who am I?" when God calls you to do something. When

you sincerely ask God who you are in response to His call, He is sure

to answer you. His answer today will be the same as it was then: "I am

with you." Moses didn't need to know all of the details. He just needed

to know that God was with him. He didn't need a play by play of the rescue plan. He just needed to know that God Almighty was with him. He didn't need to know why God chose him. He just needed to know that God was with him. All he needed to know was that with every step he would take, God was with him. While the question, "Who am I?" is healthy, the questions that followed were nothing more than a series of buts. Here's my summary of the "but" conversation.

Moses: "But who am I?"

God: "I am with you."

Moses: "But when they ask me your name, what should I tell them?"

God: "Tell them I Am sent you."

Moses: "But what if they don't believe me?"

God: "Check out what I can do with that stick of yours."

Moses: "But what about my inability to speak?"

God: "Who do you think made your mouth?"[1]

Moses was wrestling with unbelief and it shaped itself into a big fat but. He looked at his calling in light of his inability instead of looking at his calling in light of God's ability. He perceived it as too big, too much,

[1]These quotes were taken from the PSV translation (Paulette Stamper Version, 2014).

too hard, and too impossible. Before you are tempted to be too hard on Moses, consider that somewhere along the way we have all done the same thing. (98.7% of all Christians say, "But God," when the call is perceived as impossible.[1]) Why is it that those of us who profess Jesus as Lord and Savior and claim to believe that God created and sustains the universe no less, still immediately retort, "But God," when He calls us to do something? We do it for the same reason Moses did it. We take our eyes off of God and we focus instead on our inabilities instead of God's abilities. We focus on the impossibility of the call instead of the possibilities of the call. We quickly determine that there is no way we can do what God is calling us to do. Rarely do we take into account that our inability is exactly the point. We develop a rapid onset diagnosis of spiritual amnesia that prevents us from remembering God's faithfulness to us in the past. We forget simple truths like how God never calls anyone to do something in their own strength. Clichés like, "God doesn't call the equipped, He equips the called," sound good, but we don't really believe it. Or maybe we just believe it for everyone else but ourselves.

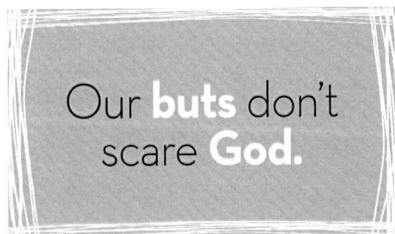

> Our **buts** don't scare **God.**

Here's some good news. Our buts don't scare God. He pa-

---

[1] 98.5% of all statistics are made up on the spot.

tiently answered all of Moses' buts. However, Moses pulled out all the stops with the grand finale but. He said, "Pardon your servant, O Lord. Please send someone else," (Exodus 4:13). Basically, Moses told God in that moment, "But Lord, I still don't believe I can do this. Please get someone else more qualified for the job." This but trumped all other buts. Moses had crossed the line. God's patience ran out and "The Lord's anger burned against Moses," (Exodus 4:14). (It is interesting to note that despite pulling out the mother of all buts, Moses still didn't get a pass from God. The Lord sent his brother Aaron to help him instead. Yeah, having Aaron as a sidekick worked out great for ya, didn't it Moses?[1])

——— FAITH AND FOCUS ———

If you are a Christ follower, then God has revealed Himself to you and placed a radical call on your life. A radical call requires radical faith. If radical faith is your goal, then know that it will demand radical focus. You can either deliberately focus on the One who calls or you can focus on the call. Focusing on the call will undoubtedly produce unbelief which often manifests as large buts of fear, doubt and/or pride. Focusing on the One who calls will keep the call in perspective. The extreme level of focus necessary to persevere in our

[1]#goldencalf

calling does not come naturally to us. I'm convinced it's tremendously difficult and challenging for our generation to maintain a prolonged focus on anything.[1] Ours is a generation that has been conditioned to focus, albeit momentarily, only on the new and shiny that produces immediate results and satisfaction. Why put it in the crock-pot when it can be thrown in the microwave? We only want to give our attention to that which makes us feel good in the moment. We certainly don't want to do or pursue anything that causes us to be fearful or the least bit uncomfortable, or even inconvenienced for that matter. Hard work, determination and perseverance have been replaced with doing only what it takes to get by and momentary pleasure pursuits. Moses didn't lead the Israelites to freedom in one day. He had to stay focused. He had to persevere. He had to keep his buts in check. He diligently pursued radical faith. God is looking for men and women in this generation who will dare to drop the buts. He is searching for those who will trust in the God who has revealed Himself as the God who sees, hears, knows and rescues. This kind of radical focus will strengthen us and empower us to go the distance our calling demands. The road won't be easy. There will be difficulties, set-backs and at times, fierce opposition. But the call to go will never be fulfilled if we can't keep our focus on the One who is doing the calling. Just because long-term perseverance is no longer the status quo doesn't mean the rewards

[2]#squirrel #shinyball #somethingsilver

for perseverance have ceased. Scripture is full of promises made to those who persevere. Galatians 6:9 is just one example:

> *Let us not become weary in doing good, for at the right time we will reap a harvest of blessing if we don't give up.*

Let's deal with our buts and relentlessly pursue radical focus, radical faith and radical belief. Our destiny awaits us on the other side of our buts.

There is another "But God" story that comes to mind. Check out John 11:17-43. (You already know I'm going to tell you to go read it.) I'm sure you are like me and have probably read this story more times that you can count. Don't let familiarity rob you of a fresh perspective. Did you notice the "But Lord," statement in this passage? When I read this story recently, I noticed it for the very first time. Jesus made a bold statement about His identity in verse 25. Speaking to Martha He said, "I am the resurrection and the life. The one who believes in me will live, even though they die; and whoever lives by believing in me will never die. *Do you believe this?"* (My emphasis.) I want to park here for a minute. I'm going to make the assumption that if you are reading this book, chances are good that you would identify yourself as a believer. If you and I were having a cup of coffee and we were discussing this passage, my guess is you would admit that you believe that Jesus raised Lazarus from the dead (which is pretty incredible in itself!) and that you believe Jesus' declaration that He is the resurrection and the life. Martha emphatically voiced her belief. In answering Jesus' direct question, "Do you believe this?" she replied, "Yes, Lord. I believe that you are the Messiah, the Son of God who is to come into the world." Bam. Now that's straight-up belief! So, before we move on, let's recap just to make sure we're all on the same page.

Jesus: "Do you believe?"

Martha: "Yes, I believe."

Pretty clear, right? After this conversation between Jesus and Martha, Jesus is deeply moved by the display of grief by Lazarus' friends and goes to the tomb. The most easily memorized verse in the Bible is found in this passage: "Jesus wept." This is such a beautiful picture of the heart of Christ being moved by the emotion around him. Never forget that God created your emotions. He knows how you feel. He is your great High Priest who is able to sympathize with you, meaning he is able to feel what you feel. Don't be tempted to believe that God is aloof and not touched by your emotion. (See Hebrews 4:15.) When Jesus reached the tomb of Lazarus, all eyes would have been on Him. No one would have expected what He said next: "Take away the stone." What a moment that must have been! Everyone's eyes must have grown to the size of bowling balls! I mean, what in the world?! Did this scene immediately turn into the most awkward moment ever? Surely everyone there must have been thinking, "Take away the *what?!* Have you lost your mind Jesus?" Martha finally spoke up and said what everyone else wanted to say, *"But Lord…"* Ah, there it is. The big but in the room. Now remember, it was just moments ago that she boldly declared her belief, and I quote, "Yes, Lord, I believe…" But throw in Jesus' command to do something that subsequently made zero sense, would have seemed highly irrational and possibly even a tad bit psycho, and suddenly we hear, "But Lord." Hmmm. Sound familiar? Seems like there are big buts everywhere, aren't there?

Just to clarify again, let's revisit Martha's confession in John 11:27. Read it out loud if you can: "Yes, Lord," she replied, "I believe that you are the Messiah, the Son of God, who is to come into the world." Humor me and read it out loud one more time if you believe it: "Yes, Lord. I believe that you are the Messiah, the Son of God, who is to come into the world."

Isn't it nuts that in one breath we can declare with certainty, "I believe!" but when called by God to put feet to our faith, to step into our calling, to embrace our destiny, our buts suddenly get in the way and we cry, "But Lord!"

But Lord, I can't speak to my neighbor about my faith! I'm too shy!

But Lord, I can't lead a Bible study. I'm not a scholar!

But Lord, I can't adopt a child. I don't have the finances to feed another person!

But Lord, I can't mentor a younger believer. I don't have anything to offer!

But Lord, I can't write a book. I'm not a writer!

But Lord, I can't go on a mission trip. I'm terrified of flying!

But Lord, _____!

May I make a strong suggestion? Commit to memory Jesus' powerful and poignant response to Martha's but in John 11:40:

Did I not tell you that if you believe, you will see the glory of God?

Here's my translation: "If you believe and will get your big but out of the way, you will see the glory of God!" It's never, "I'll believe it when I see it," but rather, "I'll see it when I believe it." *IF you believe, you WILL see.* That's an incredible promise! But wait a minute, didn't Martha just say that she believed? Don't we say the same? Looks to me like if we say we believe but then cry, "But Lord," it shines a light on the true extent and depth of our belief; or should I say our *unbelief*. We like to say we believe, and we sincerely want to believe that we believe, but when it comes right down to it, and our calling is staring us in the face, our buts stand in the way. What we are really saying is more like this: "Lord, I'll believe you when it's convenient for me. I'll believe you as long as you don't require me to do something I'm uncomfortable with. I'll believe you only when it makes logical sense to me. I'll believe you when I can trust in my own abilities." Basically, it all translates to this:

"I'll believe you as long as it doesn't require me to have radical faith."

—— DOWN WITH THE BUTS ——

I am so sick of an ordinary, boring, mundane, predictable and safe life void of evidence of a radical calling that I could puke. Honestly, sometimes I think God must be offended by our lack of desire to experience the radical calling and destiny He has for us. Jesus Christ paid the ultimate price so that you and I could be rescued from the dominion of darkness and brought into His kingdom. He has called you to a radical destiny, and as I said before, it's not something you have to wait on or hope for; your calling and destiny happened at your salvation

God wants to do the impossible **in you** and **through you.**

experience. God wants to do the impossible in you and through you. The only catch is you have to believe Him. That's it. Just believe. Radical belief in a radical God. No more buts. No more excuses. Either you believe that Jesus is who He says He is and that He can do what He says He can do or nothing at all. Hearing Jesus say, "IF you believe you WILL see the glory of God," should fire us up! Are you kidding me? That's it? We GET to see the glory of God if we will just believe. Enough with the buts already! Think about this. Because Moses dealt with his buts, he saw the glory of God. He stepped into his calling. He experienced God's power and provision firsthand. If he had not dealt with his buts, he would have missed walking through the Red Sea on dry land, eating manna from heaven, drinking water from a rock, hearing the voice of God, and seeing the Promised Land. What are you missing by not dealing with your buts? What glory are you forfeiting by not focusing on God? It's time to fix your focus on the same God that spoke to Moses from the burning bush and called him to a radical destiny that we are still talking about thousands of years later. It's time for you to fix your eyes on the God who sees, hears, knows and rescues. You have zero reason to fear. Zero reason to doubt. Zero reason to allow a big but to prevent you from stepping into your destiny. God is calling out a remnant of believers who will actually *believe Him.* Will it include you? Are you up for some straight-up crazy? Pray desperately for a radical focus on God. Pray for radical belief and radical faith. Deal with your unbelief. Confess it to God. You will never be able to step into your calling and destiny with a big but in your way.

— PERSONAL STUDY QUESTIONS —

1. Read and thoughtfully consider Genesis 22:1-19 then answer the following questions:

   a. What are the similarities between God's call on Abraham and God's call on Moses?

   b. God asked Abraham to do something that would have seemed impossible. How did God provide?

   c. How did Abraham display his trust in God?

   d. What could some of Abraham's "buts" have been? Why do you think Abraham didn't respond to God with a "But Lord" statement?

   e. Consider some of the more difficult things God has called you to do. What has been your response to Him in the past? If you remember that your God is with you, how might your future response be different?

2. Read and consider the following verses: Psalm 55:22, 56:3-4, Deuteronomy 20:4, Isaiah 12:2-3, Acts 2:25.

   a. How can these Scriptures encourage you when you feel God calling you to "go"?

   b. Consider writing a prayer to God and asking Him to plant the truth of His Word deep in your heart. Ask for a radical faith that will move you and sustain you during difficult times.

3. Glance back over the story of Moses' "but" (Exodus 3-4) and Martha's "but" (John 11). Take some time to think about your current life circumstances and answer the following questions:

   a. What similarities do you see in these two accounts?

   b. Are you where you want to be in your faith walk with the Lord?

   c. Is there anything you have felt prompted by the Spirit to do and have yet to do so? If so, why?

   d. Do you recognize any current "buts" in your life? Consider writing them down and begin praying for God to give you the courage to face them.

e. Write a prayer expressing your thoughts and feelings about the content of this chapter. Do you wish for a more radical faith? Then ask God for it and begin looking for ways to display it.

f. Consider how God responded to Moses' "buts." How does this encourage you? Consider how Jesus responded to Martha's "but." Commit John 11:40 to memory.

───── COFFEE CHATS ─────

1. Describe some reasons why followers of Jesus may struggle with "big buts."

2. Talk about the different ways "big buts" can be defeated.

3. Consider how Moses responded to God after all of his "buts." How does this encourage you?

4. What are some of the "big buts" in your life right now that you feel are preventing you from stepping into your destiny?

5. Read the following verses: Psalm 86:11, Isaiah 25:1. In what ways have you experienced God's faithfulness in your life? Describe how God's faithfulness can be key in fighting a "big but."

Questions by Mel Carroll

CHAPTER THREE

RADICAL TRUST AND CRAZY OBEDIENCE

Now to Him who is able to do immeasurably more than all we can ask or imagine, according to His power that is at work within us, to Him be glory in the church and in Christ Jesus throughout all generations, for ever and ever! Amen. Ephesians 3:20-21

"The question, therefore, is not, "Can we find God's will?" The question is "Will we obey God's will?" David Platt[1]

> If you want God to entrust you with a **radical destiny,** then you had better be prepared to be **radically obedient.**

Trust and obey, for there's no other way to be happy in Jesus, but to trust and obey.[1]

The God that split the Red Sea is the same God that wants to do the impossible in your life. The God that defeated the Egyptian army and delivered the Israelites from bondage is the same God that will defeat your enemies and bring you freedom. The God that spoke to Moses face to face is the same God that will speak to you. Do you believe this? Then you are well on your way to straight-up crazy!

I the LORD do not change. Malachi 3:6a

—— THE MAIN INGREDIENT ——

I often pray what Moses prayed, "Show me your glory!" (Exodus 33:18). I desperately want to experience God revealing as much of Himself to me that He can without it flat killing me. I want a straight-up

[1]Trust and Obey by John H. Sammis, 1846-1919. (A great old hymn. Glad I grew up Baptist.)

crazy faith that will propel me to walk steadfastly in my calling. I crave a straight-up crazy faith that will empower me to boldly fulfill my destiny. What about you? Are you with me? It IS possible, you know. We've encountered the God who sees, hears, knows and rescues. We've had our burning bush experience. Not only has God revealed Himself to us, He's called us to go and given us a radical destiny. Want to know the main ingredient in your destiny? A huge dose of *impossible*. And by impossible, I mean impossible for *you*, not God.

With God, all things are possible. Matthew 19:26b

Everything is possible for one who believes. Mark 9:23b

God delights in doing the impossible in us and through us. We all love Ephesians 3:20-21, don't we? I mean, it does sound pretty dang fantastic. God is able to do immeasurably more than all we can ask or imagine? That's amazing! I am capable of imagining some pretty radical and crazy stuff so God is really on His game if He is going to do immeasurably more than what my brain can imagine! And I don't have any trouble coming up with big crazy prayers either, so it fires

> God **delights** in doing the **impossible** in us and through us.

me up to think about God doing *immeasurably* more! However, there is more to this verse than God doing crazy big things through us. We would be amiss to overlook the second part of the verse, "according to His power at work within us." At first glance, this sounds great because it's a firm reminder that it's God's power at work in us. It's also a great reminder that we can't do anything apart from Him. However, we must also consider this: just how much access are we giving the power of God to work *within* us?

—IN ME, THEN THROUGH ME—

I absolutely love the idea and get super pumped up when I think about God doing the impossible *through* me. But the bottom line that we all too often overlook is this: God will only do the impossible *through*

> God will only do the **impossible through us** to the extent that we allow Him to do the **impossible in us.**

us to the extent that we allow Him to do the impossible *in* us. God's best work *in* us prepares us for His best work *through* us. Allowing Him to do the impossible *in* us prepares us for Him to do the impossible *through* us. The work in us is accomplished through our obedience, especially obedience that requires fierce perseverance and unyielding tenacity. So, let's talk about obedience, *radical obedi-ence.* A radical destiny cannot be separated from radical obedience. Radical obedience demands radical trust. If you want God to entrust you with a radical destiny, then you'd better be prepared to be radically obedient.

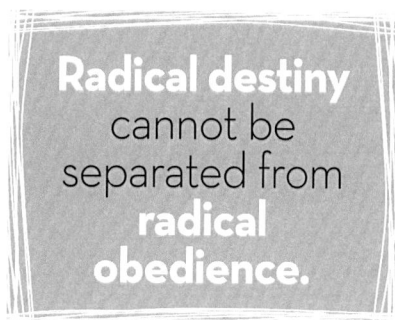

Radical destiny cannot be separated from radical obedience.

After God revealed Himself to Moses and called him to go rescue the Israelites, Moses wrestled through and overcame his big buts. He left behind the predictable, safe, routine and mundane way of life he had known for the past 40 years. I don't doubt for a second that he was fearful, but he did it anyway. He was convinced of God's promise: "I will be with you." So off to Egypt he went. His brother Aaron met him on the way and together they travelled back to Egypt. When they arrived, they shared with the elders the good news that God knew their suffering and was going to rescue them.

Moses and Aaron brought together all the elders of the Is-raelites, and Aaron told them everything the Lord had said to Moses. He also performed the signs before the people, and they believed. And when they heard that the Lord was concerned about them and had seen their misery, they bowed down and worshipped. Exodus 4:29-31

Moses couldn't have hoped for a better response. He must have been thinking, "One down, one to go!" He had convinced the Israelites that God was going to lead them to freedom; now all he had to do was convince Pharaoh to let them go. With a stick that turned into a snake, what could possibly go wrong, right? A lot, actually. Moses approached Pharaoh, spoke what God had told him to say and instead of letting the Israelites go, Pharaoh increased their labor, making things much worse than before Moses had arrived on the scene promising freedom. (You can read this account in Exodus 5.) Because Pharaoh increased the workload for the Israelites, making things ten times harder on them, they all got pretty ticked off with Moses. They blamed him for their increased hardship and wished they had never been given, in their minds, false hope.

Moses returned to the Lord and said, "Why, Lord, why have you brought trouble on this people? Is this why you sent me? Ever since I went to Pharaoh to speak in your name, he has brought trouble on this people, and you have not rescued your people at all." Exodus 5:22-23

Can you relate to Moses' obvious confusion and frustration? One minute it appeared that his obedience was paying off in a big way because the hand of God was obvious. In the very next minute it appeared like everything was falling apart because God's hand was nowhere to be seen. I can certainly relate to Moses' confusion and frustration. Years ago, God gave me a literal glimpse of where He wanted to take me. What He showed me was far from any hint of reality I had ever known. I thought one of two things had happened: either I'd had a psychotic episode and should consider medication OR it really was God and He had some pretty crazy plans in store for me... plans that included doing things that I could NEVER do on my own. I knew that time would tell if I was losing it or if what I had seen was from God. Sure enough, things began to happen that only God Himself could orchestrate. This increased my faith and I began to believe that I didn't need antipsychotic meds after all. However, not too long after things began falling into place, I was met with fierce opposition and the doors I thought were opening began slamming shut instead. And while it appeared that all the difficulties and hardships were the complete opposite of God's plan, they were in fact *exactly* God's plan. What I didn't realize at the time was that there was no way God was going to lead me down Easy Street to reach my destiny. He took me for a long trip down Bumpy Boulevard instead. I was about to get a crash course on how to persevere in obedience, even when I didn't exactly want to be obedient. I was about to learn that the trip from Egypt to the Promised Land wouldn't happen overnight. God wanted to teach me how to trust His heart even when I couldn't see or understand His hand. It was during that season of obedience that I learned how to pray prayers of desperation. I learned to trust that God was *for* me, not *against* me. Think about it. If God didn't allow hardships and opposition to come against us, how would we learn to really trust Him? If we were able to do what God called us to do with zero opposition, we would be tempted to believe we were able to accomplish it in our own strength and in our own ability. He loves you and me way too much to let that happen.

> **Trusting God** is believing that He is for you, not against you, **no matter what** your circumstances may tell you.

— PUT FEET ON YOUR FAITH —

The anger of his fellow Hebrews and the fierce opposition of Pharaoh coupled with Moses' understandable confusion and frustration cumulated in a pivotal moment for Moses. He could either say, "Forget this! I didn't sign up for this! Things were better off before I got here. I'm outta here!" Or, he could press in and say, "Lord, I don't understand what is happening right now but I believe that You called me here. I believe that You are with me. I will choose to trust You in this situation." Trusting God is believing that He is *for* you, not *against* you, no matter what your circumstances may tell you. Sure, Moses hopped on the Struggle Bus for a short time. He obviously wrestled with what was happening (or in his case, what wasn't happening). Moses had not yet learned that in order for radical faith to grow, he had to learn to trust God. Trust grows deep in the soil of hardship and uncertainty. Trust isn't really trust unless there is a real and perceived need for reliance on something outside of ourselves. If there is not a real need, trust isn't necessary. Trust is what puts feet on your faith. You can't have radical faith without radical trust.

Despite what seemed to be a devastating set-back, a "no-way José" response from Pharaoh and downright anger from the Israelites,

Moses took a radical step of obedience and chose to trust the Lord even when it didn't seem to make sense and when it looked like obedience was futile. He returned to Pharaoh and said exactly what the Lord had told him to say. Guess what God does when we do what He calls us to do, despite the overwhelming fear and doubt we may be experiencing? He does exactly what He said He would do. God is looking for men and women in our generation who will trust Him and move forward in obedience, even in the face of fierce opposition, overwhelming fear, and near debilitating doubt.

> **Trust** is what puts feet on your faith. You can't have **radical faith** without **radical trust.**

Even if it looks like God's plans are flawed. Even if it appears impossible. We can rest assured – God's plans are never flawed and nothing is impossible for Him! He knows exactly what He is doing. *He will do what He said He will do.* God will grow your trust in Him through obedience. You will never have radical faith if you are not willing to trust God, put feet to your faith, and be obedient. Because Moses didn't cut ties and run back to the desert, God grew his roots of trust deep. Moses' will and determination to be obedient grew deeper and stronger and as a result, God used Moses in amazing, incredible, and downright crazy ways. If you know anything about the future hardships, struggles and wars the Israelites would face in the desert, then you know that Moses was going to need some seriously strong roots of trust. There would be many trials in his future that would threaten to destroy him and disrupt God's divine plan for the Israelites. Radical trust and radical obedience was imperative. It is the same for you and for me.

There is a lot of talk in our generation about God-sized dreams, God doing the impossible, radical destinies and changing the world. And yes, I'm well aware that I'm writing a book talking about those exact subjects. However, none of what I say, no matter how fired up you may get, will make a bit of difference in the end if this one very important point doesn't hit home: you will never fully step into your radical destiny, never experience straight-up crazy, never display radical faith and never experience God do the impossible through you *until you first allow Him to do the impossible in you.*

Radical trust won't appear overnight. There's not a magical spiritual maturity switch that can be flipped and no magical fairy trust dust to sprinkle. You may remember that I mentioned this point in the last chapter: Our generation isn't so great at persevering. We prefer the quick, easy and painless road. The truth is this: the road from Egypt to the Promised Land is not quick, easy or painless. It requires trust, obedience and perseverance. If we stay the course, God will lead us to and through many obstacles and hardships that will result in deep roots of trust. I often pray, "Lord, grow my roots deep because when (not if) the winds of trial and hardship begin to blow, I don't want to snap in two like a twig." God is all about growing your trust in Him. He is all about you having radical faith. He is all about doing the impossible *through* you. But first and foremost, He is all about doing the impossible *in* you. You can't have the former without the latter. If you want to experience your destiny to the fullest then you have to persevere in obedience. You have to trust God even when nothing looks like you thought it was going to look. You have to trust God even when those around you walk away because they think you are a little too fanatical, a little too excited, a little too focused and a little too radical. You have to stay the course when opposition arises. You have to trust God to work out the details and show you a way when there seems to be no way. You have to trust God even when your world feels like it's falling apart. You have to trust God and never, never, ever, give up.

—— THE KEY TO OBEDIENCE ——

Here's the kicker about obedience that you and I don't want you to miss. Roots of trust will grow deep and strong in the rich soil of your obedience. The more you obey, the more you learn to trust. The more you trust, the deeper your roots grow. It's your roots of trust that will keep you from bending and snapping when life gets to be too much (aka, when all hell breaks loose), because you trust that God is in control. You trust that He is for you, not against you. You trust He will work all things for good. This kind of radical trust doesn't come naturally. It's a choice that you and I have to make.

So, if your roots of trust grow in the soil of obedience then where can you find this rich soil? It's like the one item Wal-Mart *doesn't* sell. What will motivate you to stay the course and remain obedient? How can you steadily walk in obedience when all you really want to do is throw in the towel? You will never be obedient for long if you are only being obedient for obedience's sake. You won't be able to just grit your teeth and stick it out for the long haul. Maybe you will be able to push through for a little while, but pure grit and stubbornness won't last forever. And besides, let's be honest, that's just miserable. We've all met that person who always does the "right thing" but is grouchy about it and therefore not at the top of your party guest list.[1] God doesn't want grouchy followers who manage to be obedient but miss His joy and peace. God desires followers who find delight in Him. Delight and joy come from knowing and believing that He is for

---

[1] If you are the one who never gets invited, you might be the grouchy one. Jus' sayin'.

you and not against you. So when you are faced with opposition and trials, how will you stay the course? The answer may surprise you. It may even irritate you at first because it sounds so simple. The key to obedience is found in love. Yes, love. That is the answer. A deep, profound love for your God and Savior that is rooted and established in His deep and profound love for you. If you miss loving God then you miss the entire point. It is His love, and His love alone, that will compel you to be radically obedient. It is His love that will compel you to move forward in faith and trust and to never give up.

—— WHAT'S IN YOUR HEART? ——

Take a few moments to look intently at the condition of your heart. Do you see a need to rekindle your love for God? Are you tired of gritting your teeth in obedience? What if I told you there is a place where you can go that will reignite your deep love for God? A place where you can encounter His heart and love for you afresh. There is such a place. It's found at the foot of the Cross. The apostle John tells us, "This is how God showed His love among us: He sent His one and only Son into the world that we might live through Him. This is love: not that we loved God, but that He loved us and sent His Son as an atoning sacrifice for our sins," (1 John 4:9-10). Scripture is clear.

We love God because He first loved us. And where was God's love perfectly displayed? On the Cross when Christ became our atoning sacrifice. If you really want to deepen your love for God and rekindle your love and passion for Jesus, the best and only starting point is at the Cross. Let me be clear. If straight-up crazy is your desire, if you long for radical faith, if you want to live out your destiny, the only starting point is at the Cross. I encourage you to take time to remember the moment you came face to face with the God who sees you, hears you, knows you and rescues you. Meditate on the sacrifice of your Savior, Jesus Christ.

> *For Christ's love compels us, because we are convinced that one died for all, and therefore all died. And He died for all, that those who live should no longer live for themselves but for Him who died for them and was raised again. 2 Corinthians 5:14-15*

When you become convinced of His love for you, you will no longer want to live for just yourself. Guess what no longer living for yourself looks like? It looks like radical trust and radical obedience. Love for Christ, because of His love for you, will compel you forward in obedience – even when it's difficult, even when it seems to makes zero sense, even when it appears what God is asking you to do is straight-up crazy, you will be compelled to step forward in obedience, giving less and less thought to yourself and more and more thought to Jesus.

> **Trusting God** and being obedient even when it goes against everything your flesh tells you; now that's **straight-up crazy.**

When you become convinced of His amazing and crazy love for you, your whole world will change. Your entire focus will shift. You will start living a radical life for the One who died and was raised again.

Trusting God and being obedient even when it goes against everything your flesh tells you; now that's straight-up crazy. Obedience leads to trust because you experience God's faithfulness, provision and power. When you allow Him to work *in* you, He does amazing work *through* you. Moses allowed God to work in him. He was obedient by returning to Pharaoh. Therefore, God began to work through him, and through perseverance and obedience, God did some pretty darn amazing things. *Impossible things.* Impossible *is* the main ingredient in your destiny.

If it's straight-up crazy you are going for and if you are craving radical faith, then you must allow God to do His work *in* you. Growing trust. Growing faith. Growing love. Growing a will to be obedient. Growing a self-less focus and growing an others-more focus. It's when you yield to this work in you that you will begin to see God doing through you more than you could even think to ask or imagine.

Embrace the One who has embraced you. Remember the price that was paid for your salvation. I can promise you, the more time you spend meditating on the great love of your God and Savior, the more you will love Him in return. And the more you love Him, the more you will trust Him. The more you trust Him, the greater level of obedience you will display. God will do some awesome things through those who trust and obey Him. Impossible things. *Impossible is your destiny.*

—PERSONAL STUDY QUESTIONS—

1. Pray and ask God to reveal to you what unconditional trust and obedience would look like in your day to day life. Ask Him to re-mind you of some specific instances when you displayed radical trust and obedience and consider writing them down in a journal.

2. Take some time and read the following Scriptures pertaining to trust and obedience. Consider writing each of them down and reading them aloud. Choose three to memorize. Answer the questions that follow.

Exodus 14:31	2 Kings 18:5	1 Chronicles 5:20
Psalm 4:5	Psalm 9:10	Psalm 13:5
Psalm 21:7	Psalm 22:5	Psalm 22:8

What happened in each when they trusted God?

Exodus 24:7	Leviticus 18:4	Leviticus 18:5
Numbers 9:19	Numbers 15:39	Deuteronomy 6:24
Deuteronomy 12:28		Deuteronomy 28:1

Describe the outcome in each when they obeyed God?

3. Consider journaling about some reasons why you trust God. Also, spend some time thinking about why it may be difficult at times to fully trust Him. Write a prayer asking God to help grow your trust roots deep.

4. Think about times in your life when you have felt you were being radically obedient. Was it a difficult season in your life? Describe how you were able to maintain radical obedience. How did it shape your view of God? How did it affect your relationship with God? Consider what your life would look like if you had not chosen to be radically obedient.

5. Spend some time thinking about your current life circumstances. Are you trusting God in every area of your life? Are there areas in which you can deepen your trust? If so, which ones? How can you actively invest in growing your trust roots deeper? Are you being obedient in all areas of your life? Do you have an opportunity to display radical obedience? How could radical obedience change your current life circumstances?

6. Prayerfully make a list of some things that you believe are impossible for you. Write a prayer and ask God to reveal to you how trust and obedience can move those things from impossible to possible.

———— COFFEE CHATS ————

1. What does radical obedience mean to you?

2. Describe the obstacles in your current life that make radical obedience seem unachievable.

3. Describe a time when you trusted God and experienced a positive
   outcome. What did you learn from the experience?

4. Describe a time when you did not trust God and the outcome was
   not positive. What did you learn from the experience?

5. Has there ever been a time that you doubted God's love? If so,
   why?

6. Describe a time when you experienced the love of God – it can be
   a small thing or something really big.

Questions by Dene Nidiffer

CHAPTER FOUR

CRAVING The CRAZY

Do not throw away your confidence; it will be richly rewarded. You need to persevere so that when you have done the will of God, you will receive what He has promised. Hebrews 10:35

"Lord, if it's You," Peter replied, "tell me to come to You on the water." "Come," He said. Matthew 14:28-29

"Faith is deliberate confidence in the character of God whose ways you may not understand at the time." Oswald Chambers[1]

"By nature, worship is not some performance we do, but a presence we experience." A.W. Tozer[2]

—— CRAVE THE EXPERIENCE ——

I should not be surprised that ever since I started working on a book about radical faith that I've had a thousand opportunities to either display it or freak out and panic. Just this morning, I wrestled with the temptation to freak out over it...*again*. I mean, should I really be surprised that God has put me in a position that requires radical faith? Or that I'm in over my head? Or that I can't do what He's asked me to do? I'm left with a choice. I can have faith that God will give me what I need to do what He has called me to do or I can panic and lose my mind. And did I mention panic? Reality tells me that I have a deadline looming over my head. I hear voices reminding me that I'm not a writer, tempting me to believe that I have nothing to say, and that there are plenty of other people who are more gifted and have something worthwhile to say and can say it better than I can. Then there are also the dreaded "What if?" questions. What if God really didn't call me to do this? What if it sucks? What if no one reads it? Believing these voices is one option I have and a familiar option at that. I'd be lying if I said I hadn't chosen this option before. But what if today I made the conscious decision to go the way of faith instead? What if I choose to believe that God really did call me to do this? What if I choose to believe that He will give me the words He wants me to convey to you?

What if this is an opportunity for me to push through in obedience and trust that God will be God and faithful to give me what I need? What if God will use this for His glory? What if God's call and His truth trump my reality? Here's what it boils down to for me. *I want to experience God.* I don't want to spend the rest of my life just reading and hearing about God doing awesome things in and through other people. Don't get me wrong; I love hearing about what God is doing in other people and how He is moving through others. I love hearing about God doing impossible things. But frankly, I'm tired of just hearing about it. I want in on some of that action. Don't you?

— BIG STEPS, STRONG ARMS —

By now you probably think that Moses is the only person in the Bible I'm fond of. Not true. One of my other all-time favorite guys is the apostle Peter. You have to admit, what kind of terrible book on radical faith would this be if it didn't include the story of him walking on water in Matthew 14? I'm sure you are familiar with it and have probably heard it taught a bazillion times. Hopefully you're not tired of it because it's a pretty dang fantastic example of radical faith. There's nothing about this story that I don't love. (Now would be a great time for you to read it. You're not surprised I would say that now, are you?) I love how Jesus deliberately sent the disciples out in the boat without Him. I love that He waited until just before dawn before He headed out to join them. And I never get tired of reading how *He walked on water!* The One who created water gets to walk on it if He wants to, you know. There's no rule of nature that He doesn't get to break if He so desires. I'm absolutely convinced that Jesus was having fun that night. Surely He grinned when He heard the disciples scream like schoolgirls. A friend of mine is terrified of spiders. Yesterday I had the immense pleasure of witnessing her do the funniest scream and dance routine I've ever seen when she discovered a spider on her shoulder. It was quite hilarious.[1] That's how I picture the disciples' reaction when they saw Jesus and thought He was a ghost. I don't know how He could have kept from laughing. I love to try and visualize the look on Peter's face when the idea of getting out of the boat first began brewing in his mind. I sure would have loved to witness him climbing over the edge of the boat, timidly putting one foot at a time in the water, slowly and carefully. I've taken some pretty big faith steps in my life but none that compare to literally stepping out of a boat and onto water. It gives me hope when I remember that Peter was human just like me. Most people I know tend to identify with him more so than any of the other disciples. I think it's because we can readily relate to Peter's frequent tendency to act before thinking and to speak before listening (or is it

[1] Thank you Bekah for the laugh. Your little dance routine is forever embedded in my frontal lobes.

just me?). We don't know how long Peter cruised along on top of the water before he freaked out. Poor Peter. No one will ever tell this story without telling the part about him sinking. Sad for him but the truth is, there isn't another illustration in Scripture that does a better job of teaching the importance of keeping your eyes on Jesus so you won't sink. It's so cliché, but so true. Peter did take his eyes off of Jesus and he did begin to sink. Literally. I get a huge smile on my face when I picture Peter crying out to Jesus to save him and Jesus reaching down and grabbing ahold of him, pulling him back up to safety. This may be slightly weird but I love picturing the hand and arm of Jesus in that moment. Imagine the pure physical strength it would require to lift a grown man out of the water with just one arm. When Jesus reached out and caught Peter, the muscles in His arm would have tightened and the veins would have quickly filled with blood. This feat took sheer physical *human* strength. Let's just pause here for a minute to allow what happened in this scene really sink in (no pun intended). *This was Jesus. He is the exact representation of the Father. He is the image of the invisible God. He is the Word that became flesh.* There are many verses in the Old Testament where the writers talk about the hand of God and His powerful arm. Here's just a few of my favorites:

Surely the arm of the Lord is not too short to save, nor His ear too dull to hear. Isaiah 59:1

Remember that you were slaves in Egypt and that the Lord your God brought you out of there with a mighty hand and an outstretched arm. Deuteronomy 5:15a

Right there in the middle of the lake, we see the *literal* hand of God *literally* save. Oh man, *I love that!* No matter what your circumstances are, no matter how long you have had your eyes off of Jesus, if you cry out to Him then He is sure to save. He is eager to reach out His hand and pull you back to Him. That never gets old, does it?

WORSHIP ROOTED IN EXPERIENCE

But wait, there's more! There's an important part of this story that I don't want you to miss. When Jesus and Peter climbed back into the boat, Matthew tells us that "those who were in the boat worshipped Him, saying, "Truly you are the Son of God," (Matthew 14:33). That's no big surprise, is it? Of course they did! They had just witnessed something spectacular. Jesus showed up and turned an ordinary scene into an extraordinary one. Surely their jaws were still dropped. Not only had they witnessed Jesus walk on water but their buddy Peter had done the same. It makes perfect sense that these men would have erupted in spontaneous worship and rightly so. But here's the kicker. Here's the point I don't want you to miss. The boys in the boat worshipped Jesus because of what they had *witnessed*. However, Peter's worship was because of something entirely different. He worshipped Jesus because of what He had *experienced*. Big. Difference. Consider this: If the other disciples had wanted to get out of the boat and had asked Jesus to call to them, wouldn't He have called to them too? Of course He would have! There's no way that Jesus would have stopped any of them from getting out of the boat and walking on water that night *if they had just asked.* He wasn't reserving that moment especially for Peter. Peter wasn't any more special than the rest of them. But Peter was the only one who craved the experience. He was the only one who was willing to trust the Lord then put feet on his trust and step out of the boat. He was the only one who displayed the desire for Jesus to not only do the impossible *in* him, but *through* him as well. Peter was the only one that night who craved straight-up crazy.

— GIVE ME SOME OF THAT! —

I spent many years of my life watching others take steps of faith from the safety of my boat. I witnessed God do amazing things in and through other people. I genuinely rejoiced with them and praised God for His movement in their life. But I always felt like I was missing out on something, and I was! I was missing out on feeling the water beneath *my* feet. I was missing out having the wind in *my* hair. I was certainly missing out on the experience of Jesus doing the impossible through *me*. I was just flat missing out. Sure, it's very encouraging to be around water-walkers. It's awesome to watch them trust God, climb out of the boat and go for it. That's great and all, but I'm going to be honest with you. There finally came a point in time where it was no longer enough to be just a spectator. I wanted to *experience* it for myself! I am no longer satisfied with merely observing others from the safety of my boat. I want to experience Jesus doing the impossible in me *and* through me. I don't want everyone around me to have wet feet and wind-blown hair while I'm still just hanging out all safe and sound with dry feet and perfect

> Jesus never tries to talk anyone into **staying in the boat!**

hair.[1] *Booooring!* I'm convinced that if I call out to Jesus like Peter and say, "Tell me to come to you on the water!" then I will hear Him respond to me exactly the way He responded to Peter, "Come." Jesus never tries to talk anyone into staying in the boat!

It can go without saying but I'm going to say it anyway. Peter walking on water was impossible. But if straight-up crazy is what you are going for then you'd better expect to be faced with an opportunity that's impossible for you. Impossible is the main ingredient in your destiny. God specializes in the impossible. You can't have impossible without faith. *Radical faith.* If you choose radical faith and are willing to put feet to your trust and pursue the impossible, there will be awesome experiences waiting for you outside of the boat. That's awesome and it fires me up just thinking about it! You and I were never meant to be merely spectators from a safe boat while others are having all the fun walking on water. It's time to get out of the stinkin' boat! You were meant to be an active participant in God's divine plan and His plan always includes the impossible. Your normal should never be normal. Your ordinary

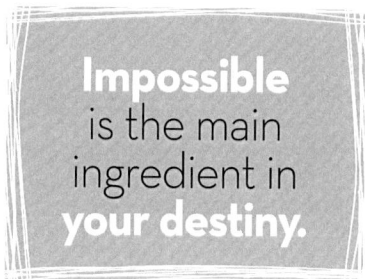

Impossible is the main ingredient in your destiny.

---

[1]Obviously I'm just making a point here. I don't honestly think my hair is perfect, although I wish it were.

should never be ordinary. Windblown hair and wet feet should be your normal. Your normal should be impossible. Heck, your normal should be straight-up crazy!

DOWN WITH NORMAL, UP WITH CRAZY

So what exactly is straight-up crazy? It's simple really. Straight-up crazy is what happens when you flat-out unquestionably believe God. I didn't say believe *in* Him. I said *believe* Him. Big difference. Believing God means you believe what He says about Himself and what He says He can do. It means you believe what He says about you and what He says you can do. Straight-up crazy is what the world should think you are when they watch how you live your life. If you call yourself a Christian, you should never look "normal" by the world's standard. *Because you're not normal.* Normal by the world's standard consists of going through life, day by day, with no real meaning or greater purpose. Normal is pursuing one's own interests and being consumed with self. Normal is being trapped in patterns of sin and not even recognizing it as sin. Normal is having no real hope or peace. We can all agree that this is normal for someone who isn't a follower of Christ. Since we are on this topic of what's normal, let me ask a question. Have you considered what has become normal for followers of Christ in our generation? In a word - comfortable. Comfortable has become the typical Christian's normal. Settled in and settled down. We get busy with the day to day responsibilities of life and we simply go through the motions. If going to church, attending a Bible study, and being in a small group were removed from the equation, our lives wouldn't look all that different from someone who isn't a follower of Christ. We are bogged down with worry, anxiety, depression, guilt, and exhaustion just like everyone else. Let's be honest. There's not a whole lot of Christians who live life outside of the boat. We've settled for a spectator seat in our comfy boats and we watch as others get their feet wet. As followers of Christ, we should not be normal by any stretch of the imagination. We shouldn't stumble around in darkness, because we have the Light of the world. We should no longer be slaves to sin, because Christ set us free from the law of sin and death. We should no longer live our lives for ourselves but live it for the one who died for us. Our normal should include believing in the God who spoke the universe into existence and calls us to follow Him. That's our normal! And to the outside world looking in, that's just straight-up crazy. When we display radical faith, we are going to look crazy. It's that simple. If we aren't willing to look crazy, then we have to ask ourselves: What exactly *are* we willing to look like? Heaven forbid we ever settle for normal.

——— HOLY DESPERATION ———

I'm actually encouraged by what appears to be a fresh breeze of desperation blowing through the Church. I sense more and more followers of Christ waking up and realizing that we weren't meant to be normal and that our lives shouldn't look like everyone else's. Just the fact that you're reading this book tells me that you are craving something more than "normal." I sense a stirring of holy discontentment in our comfortable boats and a fresh longing for wet feet. More and more I am hearing calls for the Body of Christ to repent of our selfishness and sinful ways. I'm hearing more and more leaders across multiple denominations take a stand, urgently calling the Church to pray and fast and to return to the simple Gospel message. Oh my goodness, I've been praying for years for God to bless us with a true revival in our land. I pray it comes in my lifetime. I want to be a part of a great awakening in the churches across this great nation. I believe it's beginning.

The first few drops of a revival shower are beginning to fall and I desperately pray it turns into a holy downpour. May our generation crave the crazy. May you begin to crave the crazy. May we long for God to do the impossible in us and through us. Impossible is our destiny.

RADICAL WORSHIP

Consider with me again Peter's worship of Jesus the night he walked on water. He experienced Jesus in a very real, incredible, personal way and his worship would have reflected such. It's easy to spot those who have real and vibrant worship lives, isn't it? Did you ever consider that their worship may be a response to God based on their personal experience? The other disciples missed an incredible opportunity that night because they missed what they could have had. They missed a deep and personal worship experience because they chose to be spectators instead of water-walkers. They stayed in the boat. Staying in the boat equals missed opportunities for impossible. Staying in the boat means missed opportunities for a deeper, personal worship experience. Straight-up crazy will include radical worship. I fear our Christian culture has chipped away the true meaning of worship and replaced it with the notion that worship merely consists of a few good praise songs performed by talented singers and musicians. I've heard phrases like, "Worship was awesome today!" or "Worship wasn't all that great. So-and-so can't sing," or "I didn't really enjoy worship because I don't like that song." Oh sheeze. This is so not what worship is. Worship isn't about *us* and what we get out of it for heaven's sake. It's about Almighty God. It's about recognizing, admiring and surrendering to Our Creator. It's about celebrating God's amazing gifts. It's about humbling ourselves under His authority and power. It's about His glory, His majesty, His grace, His forgiveness, and His mercy. It's about making much of Him and less of ourselves. Worship centers us where our center should be.

Don't get me wrong. I'm not implying that the other disciples didn't really worship Jesus that night. Scripture is clear, "They worshipped Him saying, "Truly you are the Son of God" (Matthew 14:33). Their worship was a genuine response to what they had witnessed. Just because they stayed in the boat doesn't mean they weren't true followers. It just means that they didn't experience all that was available to them through faith. We will always have opportunities and reasons to worship Jesus even if we choose to stay in the boat, merely because of what we are able to observe. He is constantly at work around us so we will never have to look hard for a reason to worship the King. Consider how we can look up at the night sky and see the stars He flung into place. He sustains the Universe. He created a thing called gravity and it keeps us from hurling into space. (That stunning fact alone should result in our worship!) The intricacies of a flower petal. A newborn baby. An amazing sunset. A playful dog. The sound of the ocean. Sunny days. Singing birds. An awesome bowl of chocolate ice cream. There are a million things around us that we witness on a daily basis that should evoke heartfelt worship if we are paying attention. Let's make the list a bit more personal. Jesus paid the price for our sin. We have been rescued from the dominion of darkness and brought into His kingdom. We have had a radical destiny change. We have been forgiven. His mercies are new every morning. There is no end to His grace. His love is unfailing. He calls us by name. *He sees us, hears us, knows us and rescues us.* There always exists a reason for worship. But what I don't want you to miss, is that there is also an opportunity, an invitation, for a greater and deeper level of personal worship. You can kick up your worship a notch if you will trust Jesus and take His invitation to *get out of the boat.* Then you will experience the impossible.

Your destiny includes the impossible. Your destiny will be marked by radical worship. Your destiny is rooted in your calling to go. The question is, "Will you go where you can't go on your own? Will you step out of the boat? Will you venture out in faith into areas where you will surely sink if God doesn't show up?"

Perhaps you've read this chapter and you are unsure whether or not you have ever ventured out of the boat. Maybe this will help you figure it out…

If you can personally handle everything you are doing right now, *you might still be in the boat.*

If you allow fear to keep you from trying something new, *you might still be in the boat.*

If your life looks exactly the same as it did a year ago, or five years ago, or ten years ago, *you might still be in the boat.*

If you are satisfied only hearing stories of God doing impossible things through other people, *you might still be in the boat.*

If you are bored in your spiritual walk, *you might still be in the boat.*

If you think Christianity is safe, *you might still be in the boat.*

If you think Christianity is boring, *you might still be in the boat.*

Here's the deal, peeps. If you want to display radical faith and experience straight-up crazy, *you have GOT to get out of the boat!* If you want to experience a deeper level of personal worship, nothing, I repeat, nothing can compare to walking on the water with Jesus and experiencing Him doing the impossible. Nothing this world has to offer can even begin to compare to how awesome it is to have wind-blown hair and wet feet. It's been years now, but I can still remember that as my relationship with Christ deepened, I started to understand that God wanted me to experience Him on a much deeper and more personal level. Soon after I began craving a more intimate relationship with Jesus and desiring a life that wasn't normal, I was presented with a clear opportunity to either get out of the boat or to remain in my spectator seat. I'm embarrassed to admit it but I have to be honest, I literally prayed, "Lord, when this is over can I get back in the boat?" But guess what? Once I finally climbed out, I experienced Jesus in a more real and profound way than I ever had before. I got a taste of what God had destined me for. *I experienced Him doing the impossible in me and through me.* Turns out wind-blown hair and wet feet can be super exhilarating! I can never imagine forfeiting the amazing experiences I get to have with Jesus in exchange for a safe seat back on the boat. Don't misunderstand me. I'm not saying it's always easy or exciting. Sometimes letting go of the side of the boat is dang hard. Sometimes it's very tempting to shift my focus off of Jesus and look at the ginormous waves beating against me instead. And sometimes

I have. And sometimes I sink. But Jesus always, always, picks me back up.

If it's radical faith you want, then you've got to be willing to make a move. Put one foot in the water. If it's straight-up crazy you desire then put the other foot in the water and let go of the side of the boat. If you are really wanting to experience God doing the impossible in you and through you, then I dare you to start praying this prayer:

"Lord, tell me to come to You on the water!"

Listen closely for His reply, "Come!" then go for it! And enjoy the ride because you are well on your way to straight-up crazy!

—PERSONAL STUDY QUESTIONS—

1. Read and consider Hebrews 11. Focus on the different ways bold faith manifested itself in all of the described stories. Answer these questions:

   a. Verse 16 makes it clear where these "Heroes of the Faith" had their focus. What is your focus? Is Christ and His will your goal? Is Heaven your focus or are you caught up with this world and what it offers?

   b. The faith represented by these stories is available to you. Are you taking full advantage of the faith, hope, and love offered to you by God? Are you settling for normal and average faith?

   c. What are some ways to encourage your faith and the faith of those around you?

2. In his book, *The Importance of Being Foolish*, Brennan Manning says, "We must give up our old way of life, not merely correct some slight aberrations in it. We are to be an altogether new creation, not simply a refurbished version of it. We are to be transformed from one glory to another, even into the very image of the

Lord - transparent. Our minds are to be renewed by a spiritual revolution."[1] Take a few minutes and think about your life. Would those around you be surprised to find out you are a Christian? Are you allowing the Spirit to have complete, transformational control of your life? Do you prefer to keep your life sectioned off and only give Christ control over certain areas or are you allowing Him to flood every corner of your life and being? What would happen if God had control over everything in your life, no exclusions?

3. Read Deuteronomy 11:13-15, Romans 3:21-26, Hebrews 11:1, James 2:14-17, and 1 John 5:2-5. Write down a list of what faith is and should be. Prayerfully read over your list. Is God prompting you to grow your faith in any way?

4. Meditate on the promise of Isaiah 41:10. Think deeper about the hand and the arm of God. As this truth penetrates your heart, prayerfully consider what areas of life you are trying to do in your own strength. Now, read over your list from above one more time. Consider what would happen if you applied this view of faith to the areas in your life which you have just identified. What would happen?

[1] Brennan Manning, The Importance of Being Foolish (New York, New York: Harper Collins, 205), 182.

5. As we look at our story in Matthew 14, we see that Jesus sent them across the lake. He knew they would encounter the storm, yet He still sent them. He sent them because He also knew that the storm would bring the opportunity for great faith. (Read Romans 5:3-5!) All the disciples were in the storm, but we have already learned that Peter was the only one in the boat who craved the experience of great faith. How do you allow storms to grow your faith instead of shrinking back? As a community of believers, how can we better support each other when times of "faith growth" come?

6. Before the storm came, it was smooth sailing. When God calls us in a certain direction, it may start off smooth. When things get rough, and they will get rough, how does your faith respond? Do you try and return to shore as quickly as possible? Or do you wait with confidence on the Lord? Are you willing to take the radical steps of faith when Christ calls to you in the storm? What makes those steps hard?

7. Write a prayer asking God to give you courage to have a faith like those who have come before us. Explore the opportunities God may already be giving you to walk on water and demonstrate your faith.

—————— COFFEE CHATS ——————

1. What is the boat in your life? What are the areas that make you feel comfortable and safe? Are you willing to give these up if God asks?

2. What are the waves that keep you in your boat and reluctant to get out and let go of the side? What keeps you in your seat?

3. In what ways is Jesus calling to you and asking you to step onto the water and move towards Him? Are you focusing on Jesus or are you distracted by the waves?

4. Go back and read the "You might still be in the boat…" statements. Do any of these describe you? If so, what are you going to do about it?

5. Are you willing to step out in faith, even if no one else in your boat is?

Questions by Bekah Kidd

CHAPTER FIVE

GET YOUR FIGHT ON

Be alert and of sober mind. Your enemy the devil prowls around like a roaring lion looking for someone to devour. Resist him, standing firm in the faith, because you know that the family of believers throughout the world is undergoing the same kind of sufferings. 1 Peter 5:8-9

Who is like you, a people saved by the Lord? He is your shield and helper and your glorious sword. Your enemies will cower before you, and you will tread on their heights. Deuteronomy 33:29

Paul didn't come to the end of his life and say "I have danced a good dance," but "I have fought a good fight." Jim Cymbala[1]

The way I approached writing this book was to envision sitting across from you over a hot cup of coffee (today's flavor is blonde roast from

Starbucks® brewed at a perfect 180 degrees). I'd love for us to have a good heart-to-heart conversation about life - real life. Life is never simple or easy. As we grow in our relationship with Christ, we will experience some awesome things. I'd want us to talk about our mountaintop faith experiences that have drawn us closer to God and fanned our flames of radical faith. But those aren't the only conversations I'd want us to have. Let's talk about the hard times too - let's keep it real. Life can be hard. Very, very hard. Let's talk about the reality of the enemy. I know, it's much more fun to talk about radical faith and straight-up crazy. It's way more fun to talk about God doing the impossible in us and through us, especially since we just finished the chapter about Peter walking on water. That story pumps me up every time and leaves me ready to jump out of the boat and waltz across water. However, the reality is the more our faith in God grows and the more our lives start looking straight-up crazy, the more attention we will get from the powers of darkness. I don't bring this up to scare you. We certainly aren't meant to live in fear. But let's not live unaware either. Thankfully, God's Word is not silent on this subject matter. It gives us a clear warning of the enemy's schemes and details God's perfect battle plan for us to follow.

———— WHAT'S REALLY UP ————

I'm immensely bothered by statistics that paint a very dark and seemingly hopeless picture of our moral decline. Let me clarify. I'm not simply talking about what's happening in Washington, D.C. or in Hollywood. I'm talking about what's going on in the Body of Christ, in our neighborhoods, families and homes. The Church is undergoing a direct onslaught of the enemy. More and more we are becoming indistinguishable from our lost and unbelieving neighbors. Here are just some of the statistics that should be getting our attention.

- 70% of men ages 18-34 visit porn sites in a typical month (www.assests.marshill.com, accessed July 2014).

- 90% of children ages 8-16 have viewed porn (www.assests.marshill.com, accessed July 2014).

- The largest consumers of porn are boys ages 12-17 (www.assests.marshill.com, accessed July 2014).

- 1 in 6 women struggle with porn addiction (www.assests.marshill.com, accessed July 2014).

- For every 10 men in church, 5 are struggling with porn (The Call to Biblical Manhood, Man in the Mirror, July 2004).

- 40 million adults suffer from an anxiety disorder (www.adaa.org).

- 1 in 10 Americans suffer from depression at one time or another (www.healthline.com).

- Marijuana is the drug (other than alcohol) most commonly abused in the US by individuals over the age of 12. Prescription pain killers are second. (www.addictionhope.com).

- 12 million Americans abused prescription painkillers in 2010, while roughly 15,000 die annually from overdosing on such drugs (US Centers for Disease Control and Prevention).

- Each year in the U.S., nearly 85,000 people die from alcohol related causes (www.niaaa.nih.gov).

- Every 2 minutes, another American is sexually assaulted. 44% are under the age of 18, 80% are under 30 (www.victimsofcrime.org).

My goal is not to depress you with these statistics. (It would be counter-productive if I actually *raised* the depression numbers.) My hope in sharing these statistics is that we will be brave enough to start talking about what's really going on in our lives. My hope and my prayer is that we will learn how to fight the enemy - and I mean *really* fight.

> *Finally, be strong in the Lord and in His mighty power. Put on the full armor of God, so that you can take your stand against the devil's schemes. For our struggle is not against flesh and blood, but against the rulers, against the authorities, against the powers of this dark world and against the spiritual forces of evil in the heavenly realms. Ephesians 6:10-12*

——— THE REAL ENEMY ———

We need to be reminded of the truth in this passage from Ephesians. Our fight is not against flesh and blood. When we are hit with the harsh realities of life, it can be easy to forget what God's Word tells us about the real enemy. For example, the wife who has a husband addicted to internet porn can easily begin to believe he is her enemy. If the real enemy can convince us that our loved one is the enemy then he will succeed in getting us to turn against each other and destroy each other - *which is exactly his goal.* This is one of the greatest

> We have a **real enemy.** His name is **Satan.**

weapons in the enemy's artillery. Oh my goodness, it is vital for the Body of Christ to wake up to the enemy's schemes. Your brother or sister in Christ is NOT your enemy. We have a real enemy. His name is Satan. Let's remember that and learn how to unite *together* so he will be defeated!

I'm not even going to try and hide it - this subject fires me straight-up. I am so stinkin' tired of watching the lives of those around me be slowly destroyed and relationships come to ruin because we have turned against each other instead of coming together to fight the real enemy. Well, no more! Not on my watch. I will stand on the tallest mountaintop and declare with the loudest voice the liberating and victorious truth of the Gospel. Our God saves! Our God rescues! Our God heals! Our God restores! He is our only hope of defeating the real enemy. Will you join me? Let's resolve to call on the name of the Lord Jesus Christ and wait for His response in full expectation.

Recently during a conversation with another believer, I listened as she described her current life circumstances. She was experiencing some hard blows and sadly they had taken their toll. Any hope that her life could be full of joy had vanished. She believed that she was destined to always struggle. There wasn't even a glimmer of belief left that her life had purpose or that God had called her to a radical destiny. Dire circumstances had stolen her hope and zapped her strength. She was simply unable to see beyond her pain and disappointment. As she spoke, a picture of what was happening began to form in my mind. I saw a large battlefield filled with wounded soldiers. Some were lying injured on the ground and some were limping around with significant, life-threatening wounds. The helmets and breastplates meant to protect them in battle were lying scattered about them. The shields and swords meant to defend them against the enemy's blows were no longer being used. The enemy was proudly walking around taunting the injured, convincing them the battle was over. They believed he had won and they had lost.

Sadly, I've seen this scene play out more times than I can count. The battlefield is full of believers who are convinced they've been defeated. One soldier believes his addiction is too powerful to overcome. Another believes her marriage is over. One believes there is no hope for a rebellious child. The sounds coming from the battlefield are all too often cries of pain and defeat rather than shouts of praise and victory over the enemy.

As I write this chapter, I have two types of readers in mind. The first one is like the one just described: a deeply wounded soul laying on the battlefield and bleeding out. If that describes you, you're probably wondering why you even picked a book about radical faith. You may feel like you are barely hanging on to what faith you *do* have, let alone having radical faith. If that's you, please don't stop reading now. I believe with all my heart that now is your time to stand up on the battlefield and reclaim your faith. Stick with me, will you? I believe you will be empowered and encouraged by God's Word.

The other reader I have in mind is the one who has resonated with the central message of this book. You strongly desire a life that's straight-up crazy and are striving towards a radical faith. You want God to do impossible things in you and through you. If that describes you then please hear my heart: your awareness of the battlefield and your ability to see your fellow injured soldiers is of the utmost importance. If you are standing firm, will you be willing to help others regain their ground? You were rescued so you can go rescue – *it's your calling.*

You and I won't escape this battle. And in case you are wondering if this chapter even applies to you, let me assure you it does. If you are a follower of Christ, you are a target of the enemy. No ifs, ands, or buts about it. It's a sure thing. His goal is to kill, steal and destroy (John

10:10). He will try and convince you that you are powerless, useless, and injured beyond God's ability to heal you. He may even try and convince you that you aren't in a battle and that he only goes after Christians in vocational ministry. If he can convince you to believe his lies, then he will succeed in meeting his goal.

The truth of the matter is this: The enemy is stronger than you. He is more powerful than you. He is fully capable of taking you out. (And you thought I was going to be encouraging, didn't you? Well hang on, I'm not done.) While it's true that the enemy is more powerful and you don't stand a chance against him by yourself, you must remember you are not out here on the battlefield alone. While it's true you may take some hard hits, it doesn't mean you have to remain down for the count. In fact, you can decide right now that you won't stay down. It's time to wake up and to stand up. It's time to reach out and grab those weapons that God has given you and learn to fight.

—— THE ENEMY'S A COMIN' ——

The enemy would love to convince you as a follower of Christ that you are unable to fight. He will stop at nothing to keep you from the truth that you have been given everything you need to be a strong and victorious soldier. He doesn't want you to know who you really are. His goal is to deceive you into believing you are not who God has already declared you to be. He wants you to believe your weapons aren't strong or powerful enough to take him down. *He is a liar.* Lying is his native language (John 8:44). You *totally* have weapons that can take him down. If you learn to use your weapons and fight then there is nothing, *nothing*, that he can send your way that will destroy you. Man, *I love that!*

We are going to head back to the Old Testament and dig into an incredible story that's tucked in 2 Chronicles 20. (You know what to do with this information by now, right?) It's an amazing account that beautifully illustrates how God wants His children to fight.

When word came that the enemy armies were headed their way, the people of Judah knew they were in big trouble. Their enemy was too powerful for them and their defeat and destruction was imminent. You and I need to just flat admit that we don't have what it takes to defeat the enemy of our souls by ourselves. There is no amount of self-help books, no amount of positive self-talk and no power of positive thinking that can defeat the real enemy. We simply can't do it. And when we try to do it on our own we get our butts kicked.[1] For instance if you are dealing with an addiction, the most important thing you can do is

[1] If your name is Evona Stafford and you gave birth to me, what I meant to say was "bottoms." We get our bottoms kicked.

admit that you cannot control it, manage it, or defeat it on your own. You need help – *divine help.*

As I write this, Anne Graham Lotz, the daughter of the great evangelist Billy Graham, has issued a spiritual wake-up call for Christians in our nation. She is sounding an alarm and calling on Believers across the nation to pray for a great spiritual awakening and to return to the God of our forefathers. Why? Because the enemy is having a heyday in our great nation. All you have to do is watch the evening news for about five minutes to see just how far away from God we have gone. When King Jehoshaphat was told that a vast army was approaching, he knew he didn't stand a chance. It would be like you or me receiving a death sentence with absolutely no hope of a pardon. There was nothing he or the people of Judah could do. There were outnumbered and out-powered and they would certainly die in this battle.

—————— A FIRM RESOLVE ——————

I don't think I've ever met anyone that's not been through something similar during some point in life. Maybe not quite as dramatic as having a literal army come against them but still faced with a situation that exposed their weakness, inability and helplessness. I can't think of anything much worse than the feeling of being completely helpless, knowing full well that there is nothing you can do to fix, change or escape the situation. Second Chronicles 20:3 is an incredibly powerful verse, "Alarmed, Jehoshaphat resolved to inquire of the Lord, and he proclaimed a fast for all of Judah." I like the way the KJV renders it, "And Jehoshaphat feared, and set himself to seek the Lord." *Of course he feared.* Any normal human would! The truth of the matter is this: We may *feel* like the situation is hopeless and we may *perceive* that we are powerless. But the truth is, we *can* respond to every situation that alarms us, causes fear, and exposes our weakness in the same way that Jehoshaphat responded. *He resolved to inquire of the Lord.* Let's translate this into real-life examples so we can relate. When you search the history on your husband's computer and discover a hidden addiction, *you resolve to inquire of the Lord.* When you find out that your child is addicted to pain killers, *you resolve to inquire of the Lord.* When you find out your spouse has been unfaithful, *you resolve to inquire of the Lord.* When the doctor's report is worse than you thought, *you resolve to inquire of the Lord.* When you receive sudden and devastating news of the unexpected death of a loved one, *you resolve to inquire of the Lord.* When you finally admit the truth about your own addiction, *you resolve to inquire of the Lord.* When your child tells you he or she is gay, *you resolve to inquire of the Lord.* When you suddenly lose your job, *you resolve to inquire of the Lord.* We must make the decision to inquire of the Lord *before* the enemy advances against us. As our radical faith grows, we make the decision that no matter what may come our way, our response will be to run *to* God and not *from* God. Our response will directly reflect how deep our trust roots are. If we trust that God is for us and not against us, our trust roots will be strong and deep. When we are on the receiving end of a blow from the enemy, we won't snap in two. Our response will be to immediately cry out to the One who is holding us in His hands.

> If we **trust** that God is for us and not against us, our trust roots will be **strong and deep.**

SHARE THE CRAZY

Jehoshaphat didn't just resolve to inquire of the Lord, He also proclaimed a fast for *all of Judah.* What an incredible lesson that every follower of Christ needs to take to heart. *We are not meant to take on the enemy by ourselves.* Ever. And yet all too often, this is exactly what we do. Did you know that isolation is one of the enemy's primary goals for you? He gains significant ground when you pull away from others during an attack? Is it always easy to share what's going on with others? Of course not. No one wants to grab a megaphone and announce that their husband is addicted to porn or that they are addicted to pain killers or that they secretly suffer from nightmares because of past trauma. And I'm certainly not suggesting that you *should* announce it to the entire world. However, I am suggesting that we *must* be very deliberate about cultivating authentic relationships with other believers who will walk alongside of us, pray with us and fight with us when the enemy turns up the heat. Straight-up crazy and radical faith cannot and will not happen in a vacuum. Crazy was meant to be shared.

> Straight-up crazy and radical faith cannot and will not happen in a vacuum. **Crazy was meant to be shared.**

While I'm at it, let me address the topic of fasting. Fasting is not the first thing we typically think of doing when we get the wind knocked out of us, is it? Maybe it should be. And by maybe, what I mean is, we really need to put fasting at the top of our "Ways I can display that I'm desperate for God because I have no idea what to do" list. *Fasting is the best way to display to God that we are desperate for Him.* I heard one of my favorite pastors say, "When you reach a new level of need it's time to reach a new level of prayer."[1] Nothing says a "new level of prayer" like fasting does. When we say to God with our actions, "I am more desperate for You than I am for food," we are displaying to God that we mean what we say. He responds to our displays of desperation. When we touch God's heart, His hand will follow.

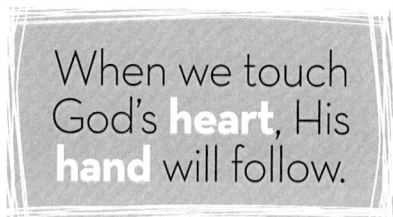

> When we touch God's **heart**, His **hand** will follow.

——— SWINGING THE SWORD ———

Faith. Straight-up crazy, radical faith. It is possible. So where does it come from? Romans 10:17 states, "Faith comes by hearing and hearing by the word of God" (NKJV). Are you looking for a sure-fire way to propel your faith into *radical* faith? *Get in the Word!* Sadly, I don't know too many Christians who make time to get into God's Word. We tout that we're too busy but somehow we still manage to find the time to keep up with people we don't even like on Facebook. I've heard Christine Caine say, "Get your face out of Facebook and get your face in *the* Book." I concur![2] We can't expect to stand our ground against the

---

[1] Pastor James MacDonald. Dude can preach the Word!
[2] I love me some Christine Caine!

enemy if we don't know the Word. Jesus Himself fought Satan with the Word of God when He was tempted in the desert (Matthew 4:1-11). If that's how Jesus fought the enemy, shouldn't we be following His example? My sweet mom always taught me that "there is power in the spoken Word."[1] That's obviously what Jehoshaphat believed. His prayer in verses 6-12 began with a bold declaration of who God is and what He had done. The Word of God is called the sword of the Spirit in Ephesians 6:17. When we meet the enemy head on with the sword of the Spirit, it strengthens our faith and reminds us of God's strength and power. Speaking the truth of the Word is like picking up a double-edged sword. Jehoshaphat wasn't reminding God of who He was and all He had done for them because he feared God had somehow forgotten and needed to be reminded. God is very well aware of who He is and what He has done. He certainly doesn't need a reminder from us. So then why bother stating these truths out loud? Picture your faith as a flame of fire. When the enemy attacks, he does his very best to put out your fire. In fact, that is his primary goal – to shake up and destroy your faith in God. However, when you speak out loud the truth of God's Word, it's like pouring gasoline on your flame. *Nothing will ignite your faith like speaking the very Word of God.* No matter what the enemy may use to try and extinguish your flame, he has no chance of doing so when he is up against someone who knows how

---

[1] Not only is she amazingly sweet, she makes the best biscuits ever.

to swing their sword. Allow me to pause here and say something that is easy to say but not always easy to hear: *You can't swing a sword you aren't familiar with.* It would be like me showing up to a gun fight when I've never fired a gun in my life - it probably will not end well for me. We have to be familiar with our weapon if we are going to be able to use it in the heat of a battle.

More Christians end up wounded, beaten and lying on the battlefield simply because they didn't know how to wield the sword. I've watched it happen time and time again. So let's talk in practical terms. What exactly does this look like? For convenience sake, I'm going to stick with the example of the wife who finds out her husband is addicted to pornography. The enemy will take advantage of this situation and will shoot flaming arrows at her that may sound something like this:

> *"If you had been a better lover, this wouldn't have happened."*

> *"You are not desirable."*

> *"You will never be beautiful enough."*

> *"Your marriage is over."*

> *"You will never be able to forgive him."*

The enemy's goal is to destroy the faith of this wife and rob her of all hope. He wants to leave her wounded and bleeding on the battlefield. *But that's not how it has to end.* Armed with the sword of the Spirit she can and will remain standing firm in the heat of the battle because Scripture tells her that…

She has been declared by God to be enough,

He has made her beautiful,

God can heal any broken marriage,

Forgiveness can come through the power and grace of Christ, and

Her husband is not her enemy.

For every arrow the enemy shoots there is a powerful truth to bring it down. My pastor said something once that I will never forget. It changed the way I communicate with my husband when I get upset and am tempted to react in anger. He said, "When you fight with your spouse, the enemy is standing in the corner cheering you on."[1] This always reminds me that if I believe my husband is my enemy then the real enemy has already gained significant ground. That just flat ticks me off – in a good way. Because if I remember that, it makes me determined to fight *for* my husband, not *with* him.

[1] Thanks Dr. Gary Johnson!

Learning the truth in God's Word and speaking that truth *out loud* is the best way to fight against the enemy's attacks - no question. Let me ask you a question. What are your eyes fixed on? You may remember that in chapter two we talked about our big buts. I made the point that if we take our eyes off of God we will succumb to big buts of unbelief, fear or pride. Jehoshaphat and the people of Judah were in a perfect position to take their eyes off of God and end up with a huge but. When they received the news of a vast army approaching, they could have easily retorted, "But we can't win this fight! But we are outnumbered! But we are going to be slaughtered!" Thankfully, that's not how the story went down. They kept their eyes where they were supposed to be:

> *For we have no power to face this vast army that is attacking us. We do not know what to do, but our eyes are on you. 2 Chronicles 20:12*

When our eyes are fixed on the Lord, we remember who He is and we view our enemy in the light of God's truth. When we look to the Lord, we are reminded that He is God, He is in control, He is all-mighty, all-powerful and all-knowing. He has not forgotten or abandoned us, He is with us, He is sovereign and He is *for us and not against us.* Mark this: ONLY when our eyes are fixed on God will we see the enemy clearly and recognize his schemes.

—————— WAIT FOR IT... ——————

I love what happened right after Jehoshaphat prayed. Everyone just stood there. That's it. They just stood there. Scripture gives no indication for how long. We just know that they stood there. It could have been for one minute, five minutes, or five hours - we don't know. All we know is that they waited. *Together*. They stood there before the Lord. Man, I love that picture. They had no idea what to do, admittedly so. They were outnumbered, admittedly so. So what did they do? They stood there before the Lord. There is a time to cry out to the Lord and then simply just wait before Him. We need to understand what waiting is and what it isn't. Waiting isn't passive. Waiting isn't weak. Waiting signifies *trust*. When you and I make the decision to wait on the Lord, we are displaying that we trust He will answer and move on our behalf, *in His time*. Waiting is one way we can outwardly and practically display our trust that God is for us and not against us.

And speaking of waiting, you get to exercise this skill right now. We are just getting started in this story and there is a ton more I want to share... in the next chapter!

— PERSONAL STUDY QUESTIONS —

1. We are not to live afraid – but we cannot be unaware of what the enemy is doing. Read 1 Peter 5:8. What is the enemy up to?

2. Take comfort in knowing that you are not alone in this fight. Read 1 Peter 5:9. How do we resist the enemy?

3. This chapter suggests we call on the name of the Lord Jesus Christ and wait in full expectation. Read another example of this in Exodus 14:13-14 and answer the following questions:

   a. What three directions did Moses give the Israelites as they faced destruction by the Egyptians?

   b. What did he promise the Lord would do for them? Do you trust that God can do the same for you? Why or why not?

4. Read Ephesians 6:10-17. Our struggle is against who? List the various parts of the armor of God and what each one stands for. Which of these weapons are you currently using? Which ones do you need to add to your daily living?

5. Another way to show God you choose Him as your help in this battle is to fast. Read Matthew 6:16-18 to see what Jesus Himself had to say about fasting. Notice that He says, "When you fast..." Also – a reward is mentioned. What are some ways that God might reward you? (Spiritual rewards.)

6. Nothing will ignite your faith like speaking the very Word of God. See what Jesus says about it in Matthew 4:4. We live on every word of God! It is how He teaches us. Read what 2 Timothy 3:16-17 says about Scripture. Note that God uses it to thoroughly equip us for every good work!

——— COFFEE CHATS ———

1. Who is your enemy? Describe a current battle you are facing or have recently faced.

2. Where do your weapons come from?

3. What can you do differently to ensure your weapons are ready? Remember, if you learn to use your weapons and fight, then there is nothing, nothing, that the enemy can send your way that will destroy you!

4. What is the advantage of being united with other believers in your battle?

5. Besides being in the Word, being united with other believers, putting on the armor of God and standing firm in your faith, what else can you do in this fight against evil?

6. Just a reminder: Keep your eyes fixed on God!

Questions by Carla Abbott

CHAPTER SIX

CRANK UP THE VICTORY TUNES

Be on your guard; stand firm in the faith; be courageous; be strong. Do everything in love. 1 Corinthians 16:13-14

"God calls us to take risks, to live fearlessly, and to be bold. He never said it'd be easy, but He promises that it'd be worth it." Christine Caine[1]

— THE BATTLE IS FOR REAL, YO —

If you're human and breathing, then you will battle the enemy. There's no escaping this tango. Either we learn how to fight in the strength of the Spirit or we will be defeated. You can probably tell based on the last chapter that I feel strongly about this subject. Maybe it's because I have watched too many followers of Christ take some hard hits and end up believing their injuries are beyond God's ability to heal. They've fallen for the lies of the enemy and believe they are down for the count. We must remember that God has equipped us with every-thing we need - not only to do what He has called us to do regarding our destiny - but also with everything we need to fight the enemy. We need not end up wounded and bleeding on the battlefield. Are we in a battle? Yes! Is the enemy going to aim fiery arrows at us with a fierce determination to kill, steal and destroy? You bet. Are we powerless against his attacks? *Absolutely not.* No way, no how, not even. Praise God, He has made a way for us to fight - *and win.* Why is this so im-portant? Why am I so desperate to make this point? Because it's like this: I believe beyond a shadow of a doubt that you have been called to a radical destiny *and* that God wants to do the impossible both in you and through you *and* that you were rescued so you can rescue others. I've prayed desperately for every single person reading these words to fully embrace these truths. It's also important for you to know that I'm not the only one who believes the truth about who you are and your calling. *The enemy believes it too.* While we may wrestle with doubt, the enemy never questions the validity of your destiny. He knows you've been called. He knows God is for you and not against you. He knows God has equipped you to rescue others. He also is very aware that the more you chase straight-up crazy and radical faith the more God will do the impossible in you and through you. Because of this he will stop at nothing to try and prevent you from living out your destiny. That's why he takes his best shot at bringing you down. If he can convince you that you have been too wounded in the battle and that your injuries are beyond God's ability to heal, he will successfully prevent you from living out your calling and your destiny. Don't let this scare you. If you stand firm against his attacks, your radical faith will send shock waves through the kingdom of darkness that will effect generations to come. Oh my goodness, this makes me want to holler out loud! We can't afford to fall for his lies! We have to wake-up! It's time we unleash some straight-up crazy and really fight! There is way too much at stake for us to stay "normal." Too many lives are hanging in the balance. Too many marriages are on the verge of collapse. Too many relationships are at risk of destruction. It's time for us to rise up and fight. It's time for us to take our wounded fellow believers by the hand and help them back up on their feet and fight the enemy with them side by side. We cannot leave our fellow injured believers behind. We're in this together.

I want to pick up where we left in the last chapter. After the people of Judah called on the Lord, they waited. When you actively wait on the Lord and His timing, you are demonstrating your trust in God. Only good can come out of active waiting. The God who hears answered their desperate cry. And boy, did He ever answer. You might want to pause here for a minute and refresh your memory by re-reading 2 Chronicles 20. It won't hurt you to read it again even if you remember it. It's some seriously good stuff.

—————— IT IS WHAT IT IS ——————

The words in 2 Chronicles 20:15 are words I desperately want you to take to heart; "This is what the Lord says to you: Do not be afraid or discouraged because of this vast army. For the battle is not yours, but God's." That sounds crazy, right? But isn't "crazy" what we are going for? Consider this important fact: God didn't minimize the threat or downplay the reality of what they were facing. Sometimes it's helpful to consider what God *doesn't* say. He didn't say to the people, "Don't worry about it you guys, it's not as bad as you think. That army isn't as big and powerful as you think it is. You've totally got this! You just need to have more confidence in yourself!" The sheer truth was that the army coming against them *was more vast and powerful than they were.* God doesn't deny reality nor does He want us to. Do you want to know what I glean from this portion of the story? *We can be authentic about our battles.* No more hiding. No more acting like everything is okay. No more pretending that we don't have problems. No more brushing things off and acting like it's no big deal. This is real life we are living. This isn't a dress rehearsal. He doesn't want you to pretend your marriage is okay when really it's in shambles. He doesn't want you to live in denial of past abuse. He doesn't want you to ignore your family's dysfunction. God always calls reality as it really is and so should we. Pardon my bluntness, but if your circumstances really suck right now, the best thing you can do is to admit that they really do suck. Only when we admit the truth about our reality will we begin to hear God speak His truth to us about it.

Even though the enemy was headed directly toward them, God told the people of Judah not to be afraid or discouraged. Know why? Because our natural reaction is to be just that: afraid and discouraged. He knows our first tendency is to look at what the enemy is throwing at us and not to look at Him. I love how

> Where we **look** will determine where we **go.**

patient God is with us. He always reminds us to keep our eyes fixed on Him and not on what the enemy is throwing our way. *Where we look will determine where we go.* It's during times of battle that having deep trust roots are vital. We grow those deep roots through quality time spent in prayer, intimate time spent with Jesus, and radical times of obedience. If we have deep trust roots, we won't respond to those attacks the way "normal" people would. I'm not saying our response should be emotion-less or we should turn into a zombie with no feelings.[1] I am saying that our response should be vastly different from someone who doesn't have a relationship with God. Why? Because we know and trust that He is for us and not against us. An attack from the enemy doesn't have to knock us off our feet *if* we resolve to stand firm on the truth of God's Word. When we boldly and courageously swing our sword, there is no lie the enemy will ever hiss that we cannot successfully dismantle and destroy. When we grasp this amazing truth it will change our lives. Nothing can and will strengthen our faith like learning to use the sword. I said it once and I'll say it again. If you are serious about pursuing a radical faith, *get in the Word.*

BATTLE PLANS

God always has a battle plan for His children who are being attacked by the enemy. In my own personal experience, the battle plan never looks quite how I would want it to look. I'm fairly sure this must have been how the people of Judah first felt about the battle plan the Lord laid out for them:

---

[1] Do zombies even have feelings? Seems to me probably not, but I'm only guessing.

Step One: Boldly march down and face the enemy.

Step Two: See Step One.

Say Whaaat? Didn't God just tell them that the battle wasn't theirs but His? Hadn't He just assured them that they wouldn't have to fight this one? Then why in the world would God tell them to march straight into the danger zone and actually face the enemy? That would have been terrifying! Couldn't God just zap the enemy without them ever having to leave the safety of their camp? Of course He could have. God can do whatever He wants, whenever and however He wants to do it. You may recall that we've talked about how God chooses to include us in His divine plans. He wants us to show up. In fact, He wants to take us right up to the front lines where we are looking the enemy in the eye. Why? Because He wants to do the impossible through us and *He wants us to see it, hear it, know it and experience it.* Remember the chapter on trust and obedience? We may not understand His plan, we may be scared, and we may flat not want to do it, but we trust that God is for us so we must move forward in obedience. Listen carefully. In our pursuit of radical faith and a straight-up crazy life that demonstrates God's ability to do the impossible through us, the scenario we read about in 2 Chronicles 20 is not the exception nor is it uncommon. Here's the facts: the enemy *will* come against us. He *is* more powerful than we are. God *will* send us directly into battle. We *will* come head to head with the enemy. Never, not once, will God tell us to turn around and run. We will never hear God sound the alarm and tell us to retreat. There's no need to retreat when we have been given exactly what we need for battle. *The enemy is real.* Evil is prevalent in our world and in our culture and in our neighborhoods and our homes. We are targets. Our family and our friends are targets. Our churches are a target. Our

> We cannot live out **radical faith** in a vacuum. We cannot be **straight-up crazy** in solitude.

nation is a target. The enemy is very, very busy shooting flaming arrows. The question is, are we marching boldly out to face him? Are we bringing our fight out into the light or are we keeping it hidden? The sooner we start admitting the reality of the battle, the better off we will all be. Remember what the people of Judah did when they learned of the vast army coming to attack? They gathered *together*. They prayed *together*. They fasted *together*. They waited *together*. Then God told them to march toward their enemy *together*. We cannot live out radical faith in a vacuum. We cannot be straight-up crazy in solitude. It's time we face the enemy *together*. It's time we admit the reality of the battle. And it's long past time that we as believers stand together and fight remembering that our brothers and sisters are not the enemy. The enemy is the enemy. Let's fight him. *Together.*

Let's deal with the reality of what happens when we discover the enemy is advancing toward us. The reality is we are tempted to freeze in fear and suffer from discouragement. How do I know this? It's not only because I've been in the counseling field for a while, although the personal accounts I've heard over and over testify to the validity of the statement. I know fear and discouragement are real reactions because so often in Scripture on the cusp of uncertainty God says, "Do not be afraid and do not be discouraged." Why would God say that if we weren't afraid or discouraged? We cannot help the way we feel. Feelings in themselves are neither bad nor good; feelings are just feelings. It's what we do with them that counts. If we are afraid or discouraged, we can fix our eyes on God and resolve to inquire of the Lord. We don't have to *stay* afraid and discouraged. I love the consistency of God's Word. When Moses was afraid and insecure, God told him exactly what He needed to hear, "I will be with you," (Exodus 3:12). When the enemy army marched against Judah, *of course* they were afraid! The remedy for their fear was the same as it was for Moses. God spoke through the prophet Jahaziel and said, "The Lord will be with you," (2 Chronicles 20:17). When the enemy marches toward you and your family, remember *the Lord is with you.* This truth will sustain you. This truth will give you the courage you need to march boldly against the enemy. This truth will empower and strengthen you in the most difficult and challenging times. *You are never alone.* You don't have to fight the battle alone. Your God fights for you. He gives you the strength, the power, the courage, the boldness and the confidence to not only stand firm against the enemy but also to march straight down and look him in the face. There is not a single weapon the enemy could ever use against you that will prosper. *Not a single one* (Isaiah 54:17). He is no match for the child of God who knows how to use the sword.

When you really begin to grasp that the same God who created the universe is the same God that is *with* you, you will have the confidence you need to face anything the enemy throws your way. Not confidence in yourself or your abilities, but confidence in who God is and His abilities. It always comes down to this: God is for you and not against you. Who can stand against God? Who can come against the Almighty? Who is His equal? What god is like our God? When we rehearse these truths they will build our faith! Makes me want to jump up and down just thinking about it. You have nothing to fear because *your God is with you.* You *can* march boldly to the front lines and look the enemy in the face. Resolve to stand firm. Your God is with you!

When Judah's enemies came against them, their petty differences would have no longer mattered. They united in prayer and in purpose. I bet if they had ever argued about what type of praise music to have, or what color the carpet should be, or *gasp* the role of women in ministry, or whether or not believers should drink alcohol (should I keep going? 'Cause I could go on all day) it suddenly wouldn't have mattered when the enemy came against them. How ridiculous would it have been if they had ignored the warning of the enemy's approach and continued to argue over petty differences? If their focus remained on their differences then they would have been destroyed. Um, hello? Isn't this what is happening all around us? Aren't we all guilty of this? We are too busy paying attention to things that won't make a hill of beans difference in eternity while the enemy approaches and devours our families. Our churches. Our nation. It's time for us to respond like the people of Judah. Let's come *together* in unity. Let's resolve to inquire of the Lord, to fast and pray, and march against the real enemy – *together.*

> *Therefore put on the full armor of God so that when the day of evil comes, you may be able to stand your ground,*

and after you have done everything, to stand. Stand firm

then, with the belt of truth buckled around your waist, with

the breastplate of righteousness in place, and with your

feet fitted with the readiness that comes from the gospel

of peace. In addition to all this, take up the **shield of faith,**

with which you can extinguish all the flaming arrows

of the evil one. *Take the helmet of salvation and the*

sword of the Spirit*, which is the Word of God.*

Ephesians 6:13-17

You may have noticed by now that this book is geared toward the pursuit of radical faith. (If you've missed that then I'm going to assume you have skipped everything and just started reading right now.) Don't miss the important concept of togetherness. It's shown up several times already and it's right here in Ephesians 6 too. Paul refers to the shield of faith and its job is to extinguish ALL the flaming arrows of the evil one. You read that right. ALL of them. Not just some or a few, but *all*. How? When Paul wrote this, he used the example of the battle gear worn by Roman soldiers. When he came to the shield of faith, he was describing the shield they carried when they advanced against the enemy armies. They measured up to 6 feet in length thereby functioning as a complete body shield. They were made of solid steel. Nothing was getting through those puppies. All vital organs were covered. That's cool and all, but do you want to know what's really awesome about the shields? They were made to link with the soldier's shield on their right and left sides. Once hooked together, these shields would have formed an impenetrable wall that allowed the soldiers to bravely march straight into the enemy territory. You and I are meant to lock our shields of faith with fellow believers in Christ. Then we can make significant advances against the kingdom of darkness. If we stand firm behind our shields of faith, then there's not a single flaming arrow from the enemy that can make it past our shields. We are meant to stand firm *together.*

—BATTLE SONGS AND VICTORIES—

God told Judah they would not have to fight the enemy. Yet, they were to take up their positions, stand firm, and march against them. Doesn't seem to make much sense, does it? God wanted them right there on the front lines so they would see what He was about to do. He was involving them in His divine plan. The next part of the story has influenced my pursuit of radical faith more so than any other account in Scripture: *they put the singers on the front line.* That's right. The singers. Not those most skilled in battle. Not the biggest or the strongest. Just the singers. Now that takes some nerve, doesn't it? Actually, no.

Nerve has nothing to do with it. It has everything to do with *faith*. You see, God had already told them they would not have to fight. So what did they do? They marched straight into battle *singing songs of victory*. While they couldn't yet see the victory with their eyes, while their circumstances had not changed, God had spoken and they took Him at His Word. So, they sang. They praised. They locked their shields of faith together and they advanced boldly and courageously against the enemy. All God wants from us is a song of praise. God delights when we acknowledge His power and strength over the enemy. He loves when we believe He has already fought the enemy for us - *and won*.

God used this passage of Scripture in my life a few years ago. I was in the midst of a significant spiritual battle. God had called me to do something very specific and I knew it wasn't anything I could accomplish on my own or in my own strength. As I began moving forward in obedience, the enemy pushed back. At one point every door slammed shut. There was literally nothing more I could do and yet I knew this was something God had put before me. That's when God led me to 2 Chronicles 20. It was one of the greatest tests of my faith, still to this day. I've never literally heard God's voice, but there have been a few times in my life where I may as well have. This was one of those times. In the midst of the battle, I clearly heard God whisper to my spirit, "Paulette, do you *really* believe I can do this?" I answered without hesitation, "Yes, Lord! Yes I do! But there's nothing more I can do!" Then He said to me, "Praise me. Praise me and thank me for doing this as if it is already done." *Whoa*. Please don't miss this. In my eyes, it already *was* done. All options were gone. Every door had been shut. God had made sure that there was absolutely nothing more I could do. Period. And yet, He wanted me to praise Him as if it were already accomplished. I'll be honest with you. This was *so straight-up crazy* that I didn't share it with another soul. Not a one. Looking back on it, I wish I had. I wish I'd shared this journey with a few trusted friends. But at the time I literally thought that if I had told anyone, they would have thought I was nuts. I gladly tell the story now and am reminded of it every time I read the story of Jehoshaphat and Judah. I lifted my shield of faith. I began praising and thanking God for His provision and power and victory *before* I saw it. I chose to believe it before I could see it. Oh my. Oh my, oh my, OH MY. I watched God begin to open doors that had been tightly shut. I literally watched God make a way where there was no way. It was like watching Him move a mountain! He turned every "no" into a big fat "Yes!" And all the while, I had zero to do with it. All I did was keep my shield of faith up and praise God. That was it. *And that's how God wanted it.* Because you see, all He wants from us is our faith. All He wants from us is our belief. All He wants is our obedience. He wants to do the impossible. And He wants us on the front lines to witness it. What an amazing and great God we serve!

The people of Judah sang their little hearts out and marched straight up to the enemy. Surely they were wondering the entire time how in the world this was going to work out. Surely they were scared. But they moved forward anyway. They carried the sword of the Spirit and they raised high their shield of faith. *And God showed up.* He did exactly what He said He would do. They watched with their own eyes the enemy armies turn and destroy each other. They didn't have to lift a single finger - *they only had to lift their voices.* Oh, Church! Let's lift our voices *together* in praise! The enemy has not overcome us! We can fight! We can advance against the powers of darkness and overcome! You know what just occurred to me as I wrote this? If just one of you reading these words right now began to believe that God will do what He says He will do, then it's all worth it. Because your life would radically change and it wouldn't stop there. Radical faith is contagious. And it starts with one. One person who will believe and leave doubt behind. God IS faithful. He WILL do what He says He will do. Believing Him *is* radical faith.

PARTY TIME

Before I get too carried away, I don't want to forget and leave out some of the details at the end of this story because they are way too good to overlook. Once the enemy armies had been destroyed, the people of Judah gathered the valuables that had been left behind. Don't miss this: *Judah was better off AFTER the battle than they were before!* Now if that doesn't light your fire then your wood is wet! We need to start seeing our circumstances in light of the big picture. We need to practice seeing how things can and will look on the other side of victory. Let me give you a practical example. I have a friend whose husband wrestled with an addiction to pornography. It threatened to destroy both of them and their marriage. Talk about a battle! However, my friend made the conscious decision to remember that her husband was *not* the enemy and chose to fight the real enemy instead. She fought with her sword and stood firm on the truth of Scripture. She raised her shield of faith and resolved to inquire of the Lord. Praise God – the battle is being won! And that's not the end of their story. Just like Judah, she and her husband are picking up loot! They decided to write their story down, choosing to believe that God would use it to help other couples who are facing the same battle. Their story was published and now it's encouraging and equipping countless others across this nation.[1] Now that's some serious loot! *If we stand firm, if we wield our swords, if we hold high our shield of faith, if we believe God, then we WILL be victorious!* Your radical faith will make the enemy sorry he ever messed with you. Now that's straight-up crazy!

> *So do not throw away your confidence, it will be richly rewarded. You need to persevere so that when you have done the will of God, you will receive what He has promised. Hebrews 10:35-36*

One more thing I don't want you to miss. Once this battle was over and the loot was gathered, the people of Judah gathered in the Valley of Berakah. The name literally means the Valley of Praise. Oh yeah. When we get on the other side of a battle we need to remember to throw a big *par-tay!* A big ol' straight-up crazy party because we have much to celebrate. We've experienced God doing the impossible in us and through us. We are living out our radical destiny. So, if you are in the heat of a battle, stand firm. Use your sword. Raise up your shield of faith and lock it with others who will help you sing songs of victory. And start planning your future party 'cause soon enough you'll be gathering some awesome loot!

---

[1] *Pure Eyes, Clean Heart, A Couple's Journey to Freedom from Pornography* by Jen Ferguson and Craig Ferguson, 2014. (Yay, Jen!!)

— PERSONAL STUDY QUESTIONS —

1. Read and consider 2 Corinthians 5:13-20. God uses us to tell others about Christ. We are His ambassadors to this world. Our lives are not meant to look like the rest of the world's. Do you believe that God has a radical call on your life to tell others about Christ? Are you pursuing it? In what ways?

2. Read 2 Kings 6:8-22. Read verses 16-17 again. What truths can you glean from these verses that will encourage you as you face various battles in your life? Those who are with you are more than those against you. You are not fighting alone. The truth is that the war has already been won. We stand on the side of victory thanks to Jesus Christ! Do you sometimes feel like you are backed up against a wall and there is no escape? Consider writing a prayer to God asking Him to open your spiritual eyes and to remind you that you are not alone. He is faithful and will deliver you.

3. Read and consider 2 Samuel 5:17-25. God delivered David and gave him victory just like He did King Jehoshaphat and the people of Judah in 2 Chronicles. (The Bible is full of stories of God's deliverance and ultimately it all points to His final rescue of us.)

These two passages have more in common than just deliverance. Look again at 2 Samuel 5:19, 23 and 2 Chronicles 20:3. David and Jehoshaphat went to the Lord and asked for direction and guidance. Where do you look when you are in the midst of battle? Is your first response to bring it to the LORD in prayer?

How do these accounts of God's great deliverance encourage you in your walk with the Lord?

4. Read Hebrews 12 and answer the following questions:

   a. Which faith story speaks to you the most?

   b. Which one encourages you the most and why?

   c. Is there a story of faith that makes you nervous?
      If so, why?

5. Read and consider Hebrews 13:1-3. We are to be encouraged by those who have lived lives of great faith before us. Have you ever considered what your faith legacy will be? How will the decisions you make in your battles affect your children and/or those who are coming after you? If there was a verse in Hebrews 12 that told what you had done by faith, what would you want it to say?

6. Read and prayerfully consider Colossians 3: 1-14. We are chosen and dearly loved. Our response to this should be to set our hearts and minds on things above and not on this world. We are called to die to our old selves. This can feel like quite a battle sometimes. Is there a part of your old self that is more difficult to put to death than others? Is there anything holding you back from pursing God's call? Remember, no matter what the battle may be, God can deliver you. Consider making a list of the truths you read in Colossians 3:1-14 that can help you in the heat of the battle.

COFFEE CHATS

1. How are you pursuing the radical call God has given you?

2. Do you downplay your real battles and struggles? Do you keep them hidden? If so why?

3. How do you fight your battles, with God or in your own strength?

4. Who is in your community? Who have you locked shields with? If you haven't, what is holding you back?

5. How is God calling you to respond to what you have read?

CHAPTER SEVEN

A NEW KIND of MaTh

What good is it, my brothers and sisters, if someone claims to have faith but has no deeds? Faith by itself, if it is not accompanied by action, is dead. James 2:14, 17

"Potential is God's gift to us; what we do with it is our gift back to God." Mark Batterson[1]

Let's kick up this notion of straight-up crazy a notch or two. What if straight-up crazy wasn't just something you experienced every now and then? What if straight-up crazy wasn't just a once in a lifetime Red Sea splitting moment or an occasional walking on water occurrence (as awesome as those are)? What if straight-up crazy described your life 24/7? What if straight-up crazy *was* your life? What if every single thing you believed and did displayed straight-up crazy and *required* radical faith? Sounds a little extreme, doesn't it? If you haven't fig-ured it out by now, I'm on the quest for extreme and I'm hoping you are along for the ride. It's a steady and purposeful pursuit. I'm by no means suggesting that I have arrived or that I have mastered straight-up crazy but I'm definitely on the chase. And I'm more than willing to look crazy doing it too!

Let me let you in on a little secret. The book you are holding in your hands is straight-up crazy. I haven't known what the chapters were going to be about until it came time to write them. Even when I thought I had an outline, God had a different one. This chapter is no exception. This particular chapter was born out of many hours of thinking intently about what straight-up crazy really looks like. I kept hearing my own words echo back to me, "God gives us what we need to do what He has called us to do." Reason with me for a moment. If God has called us to a radical destiny then our radical destiny is not going to have an on and off switch – it's always going to be on. So it stands to reason that if God has given us what we need to accomplish our radical destiny, then what we've been given won't wax or wane either. Basically, we always have what straight-up requires at any given moment. A radical call is a way of life. Straight-up crazy won't just describe our life every now and then; it will *be* our life. Neither will straight-up crazy grow stale or diminish with time but rather its intensity will continue to increase. After hearing all of this, the question you may be asking is, "What in the world does all of this even look like?"

If God has already given us everything we need to do what He has called us to do, then we must ask the question, "What exactly *has* He given us?" Here's the short answer: *gifts*. He has given us gifts.

Sounds too simple, doesn't it? Let me catch you before you tune me out because you think this is going to be a chapter solely about spiritual gifts. I assure you, it's not.[1] Actually, it's about everything you have. *Everything*. And how everything is given, or *gifted,* to you by God to do what He has called you to do. Or to put it into language that we have been using, God has given you the gifts you need to live a life that is nothing short of straight-up crazy and to fulfill your radical calling and destiny.

No one who desires to live straight-up crazy and pursue radical faith gets to remain in a mindset that declares, "I'm not gifted." If that describes your mentality then do me a favor and check your pulse. Right now, go ahead, check your pulse. Is your heart beating? Great! Then that means you're breathing and breathing alone indicates that you are in fact gifted. (Consider the alternative and you'll agree with me – breathing is most definitely a gift!)

There are several stories in the New Testament that stick out to me regarding gifts that I want us to look at in this chapter. One includes a little boy, at least 10,000 people, a massive need, freaked out dis-

---

[1] Not that that would be a bad thing. I'm tossing around the idea of writing an entire study on just the spiritual gifts. It's an important topic!

ciples, one small gift, and a straight-up miracle. Go ahead, grab your Bible and read Mark 6:30-44.

If you are like me at all, your first reaction to this story may include frustration toward the disciples. I mean really, dudes, how long have you been hanging out with Jesus and yet you still freaked out when He asked you to feed the masses? Jesus said to the disciples, "You give them something to eat" (v.37). The disciples responded, "That would take more than a half year's wages!" (v.37). In the original Greek language their response was, "*But Lord,* we can't feed all these people! *But Lord,* we would have to work over a half a year to be able to buy enough food! *But Lord,* what you are asking us to do is impossible!"[1] If you search the Scriptures looking for impossible scenarios you will find plenty of them, just like this one, throughout the entire Word of God. You know by now that God delights in doing the impossible in and through His children. This day was no exception. The situation wasn't looking too great. The crowd was large. The need was enormous. These facts obviously worried the disciples but Jesus certainly wasn't worried by them. And why would He be? He had planned this scene before the creation of the world. It was definitely a divine set-up. What was needed to meet the vast need had already been provided. He was just waiting for them to recognize it.

[1] *Did you really need a footnote to tell you that I made this up?*

——— FACTS AND FAITH ———

One little boy, five loaves of bread and two small fish. It all seems pretty insignificant, doesn't it? The need was ginormous and the apparent provision paled in comparison. But facts can't hinder or prevent God's movement. Impossible situations can't dictate what the hand of God can

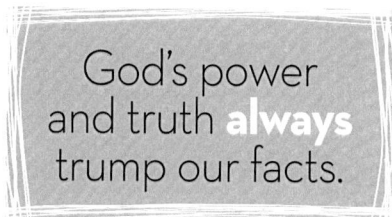

> God's power and truth **always** trump our facts.

or cannot do. Facts never have the final say-so in God's plan. Why? *Because God's power and truth always trump our facts.* God's hand is sovereign in every circumstance. No matter how big or impossible things may seem to be, He is faithful to give us what we need to do what He has called us to do. The question should never be, "Is God able?" but rather the question should always be *"Will I trust God?"* Will you step forward in trust and obedience in the face of impossible? The facts that day were undeniable: there was a large crowd of hungry people, the only food available was five loaves of bread and two fish, and there was nowhere to go and buy food, and no money to buy it even if there had been. (Even the dollar menu at McDonalds® would have blown their budget!) These were the cold, hard facts. In the moment of great need, the disciples chose to look at the facts instead of

> If He has called you to **do it**, He will bring you **through it.**

looking to Jesus for the solution. They chose panic over praise. No matter how grim, disappointing, challenging, or *impossible* a situation may be, we must remember that God will *always* give us what we need to do what He has called us to do. *The disciples didn't stop to think that the mere fact that Jesus told them to do something about it signified that He had already provided the solution.* If He has called you to do it, He will bring you through it. God specializes in doing the impossible. When you think it's over He's just getting started. He delights in doing the impossible *in you and through you.* We need to train our eyes to look beyond our circumstances. Somewhere in the chaos of our impossibilities are gifts that will bring about a solution. We may think that our five loaves and two fish aren't much but when we place them in the hands of Jesus, He will multiply them and meet the need in ways that we could have never dreamed or imagined possible.

In the hands of Jesus…
a little becomes a lot,
less becomes more,
small becomes big,
and impossible becomes possible.

This same story is also recorded in John 6:5-15. In this account we learn that Jesus asked Phillip directly, "Where shall we buy bread for these people to eat?" (v.5). I love the very next verse because it so clearly and beautifully reveals the character and heart of Jesus. It reads, "He asked this only to test him, for He already had in mind what He was going to do" (v.6). Of course He did! This hungry crowd did not take Jesus by surprise and neither does your vast need or impossible circumstance. You can take great comfort in knowing that He already has in mind what He is going to do. It was Andrew who spoke up and said, "Here is a boy with five small barley loaves and two small fish" (v.9). Andrew was the one that took it upon himself to scan the crowd to see what kind of provision he could come up with. At least Andrew didn't display a defeatist attitude - he actually looked for a solution. But he also acknowledged the facts, "…but how far will they go among so many?" (v.9). This is the attitude that most of us have toward our gifts. We may recognize we have gifts but we certainly don't see how they can meet the vast need around us. The first step is recognizing who we're dealing with.

Don't miss the fact that Jesus Christ - *God in the flesh* - had the power to immediately fill everyone's stomach by merely speaking a word if He had wanted to. This is the same Jesus that suspended the natural law of water beneath His feet, commanded the wind and the waves to be still, opened the eyes of the blind, the ears of the deaf, and raised the dead to life. Filling empty stomachs would have been a piece of cake. But as we have seen before, He chooses instead to meet the need and do the impossible *through* us. He chose to use just one little boy, five loaves and two fish to meet an enormous need. *Just one little boy. Just five loaves. Just two small fish.* Never, ever should you fall for the lie that you can't make a difference because you are just one person. *You have a gift.* Place your gift in the hands of Jesus and trust Him to apply His godly multiplication skills. Jesus + your gift offering = impossible made possible.[1]

When you are chasing straight-up crazy the need will always be greater than your ability and means to meet the need. *That's exactly the point.* If the need is not greater than your natural ability to meet it then you aren't living in the realm of straight-up crazy that requires radical faith. One of the greatest needs in your ongoing pursuit of straight-up crazy is to train yourself to see situations the way God sees them. It's usually easy to spot the need but it's not always so easy to recognize the gifts and resources God gave you to meet the need. Your gifts and resources will always appear to be insufficient (and they are until you place them in the hands of Jesus). There will be times when you

---

[1] *My editor pointed out that I'm talking about multiplication here but I use addition as an example. Well, I've never been good in math. You get the point.*

may be tempted to believe you have nothing to offer but the truth is, God has already given you what you need to do what He has called you to do.

We are all tempted at times to believe that just one person can't make a significant difference. I wonder if that's what the little boy thought with his seemingly insignificant little basket with only five loaves and two fish. But because of his willingness to step forward and give what he did have, God did the impossible and the hungry were fed. (There He goes again, doing the impossible in and through ordinary people!) In the grand scheme of things, five measly loaves of bread and two tiny fish just doesn't seem like a lot, especially when you have over 5,000 hungry people staring at you (scholars estimate as many as 15,000 when you count the women and children). But when it's handed over to Jesus – bam! The need is met. And guess who gets the glory? God does. And guess who got to experience God doing the impossible? Everyone whose need was met. And guess who got to experience God doing the impossible through them? One little boy. God is looking for followers who are willing to give back to Him what He has already given them. Which leads us to our next point; God *expects* us to do something with what He has given us.

In Matthew 25:14-30, Jesus tells a parable about bags of gold to make His point. Go ahead, you know you want to read it. I'll wait right here till you're finished.

Whether or not you realize it, *you* are in this parable. Whether you are the rambunctious dude with five bags, or the resourceful guy with two bags or the scared guy with one bag. The point is *you have been given something by God and it is your responsibility to do something with it.*

— A CHANGE OF PERSPECTIVE —

I've noticed something common in our little Christian-bubble culture. When we talk about gifts, we tend to think only about spiritual gifts. Jesus could have had spiritual gifts in mind when He taught this parable, but I believe it's about much more. He's talking about all gifts. I can hear some of you already saying, "But I'm not gifted." And what you mean is, "I can't sing. I can't teach. I can't preach. I'm not an evangelist." These statements may be true for some of you, but you don't get to check out so easily! Paul says in 1 Corinthians 4:7, "What do you have that you did not receive?" Great question Paul! Can you name a single thing in your entire life that you have that was not given to you in some form or fashion by God? Allow me to paraphrase Paul. *You don't have a single thing that wasn't given to you by God!* Don't misunderstand, I'm not saying some people haven't earned what they have through years of hard labor. I am saying that being able to work is a gift from God. If we really grasp this truth and begin to look at everything we have as a gift from God *it will change everything.* You. Are. Gifted. Therefore, *you* are in this parable. The point is not how many bags of gold you have. The point is what you are doing with the bags you have.

Allow me to go on a tangent for a minute, will you? Pursuing straight-up crazy and radical faith *will* change your life. If you have made a habit of reading multiple books on radical faith and have read every faith story in the Bible but your life still looks like it did a year ago or five years ago, then allow me to gently say, I think you've missed the point. The straight-up crazy train left the station without you. Straight-up crazy means your life *will* change. But don't lose heart - it's never too late. Straight-up crazy doesn't have to begin in the distant future; it can begin today by simply changing your perspective. If you and I begin to look at everything, *everything,* as a gift, it *will* change the way we live. Take a few minutes to consider this simple question: "*What have you been given?*"

I'm going to approach this subject by addressing some of the most commonly overlooked gifts by Christians. Let's start with the gift of material possessions. What is currently in your possession? What has God entrusted to you? We have a tendency to compare ourselves to those who have more, bigger, better and newer things than we do. Comparing ourselves to others leaves us believing we don't have anything significant to offer. We shy away from doing such and such because so and so has better _____ and _____. You can fill in those blanks with just about anything. May I challenge you to lay aside the comparison for a moment? Be willing to take an honest inventory of what you *do* have. Do you have a roof over your head? Do you have a vehicle? Do you have food in your pantry? What about a spare bedroom? Extra clothes in your closet? When you and I take an honest look at what we have been given, and we remember the parable of the bags of gold, shouldn't we respond with a straight-up crazy giving attitude? Shouldn't we begin looking for ways to multiply our gifts? Shouldn't we look for ways to bless others with our blessings? Let me just go ahead and throw this out there while I'm at it. I get that it's scary to start thinking like this. For example, I understand that the thought of opening up your home to someone who needs a place to stay can be an overwhelming and scary thought. It may mess up your routine. It could be bumpy. It will certainly kick you out of your comfort zone. *But if we are going to take Jesus seriously, if we are going to apply His words to our life, if we are going to live straight-up crazy, then we have to leave our comfort zones behind.* I'll confess something to you. I'm guilty of craving and seeking the straight-up crazy moments that are on the same scale as the splitting of the Red Sea. Those are awesome, right?! Don't get me wrong, I believe God *wants* to show Himself in those moments and He *wants* us to believe Him for the impossible. But my guess is that you are like me and you need your definition of impossible to be stretched. Impossible isn't just the Red Sea dividing. Impossible is also changing the way we think and act on a moment by moment basis. Sometimes I think changing my stubborn and selfish heart is a bigger deal for God than it was to part the Red Sea. A few years ago, it was impossible for me to imagine opening up my home and sharing my life with someone other than my husband. This whole "look at everything as a gift" really began to rock my world. God had blessed us with a home with more space than we needed. The more we thought about our home as a gift, the more we knew He wanted us to offer it back to Him and to multiply its use. Since taking that step of faith over two years ago, we've consistently had someone living with us. At one point, we had three young ladies with us at the same time and hey, that's *a lot* of estrogen under one roof! Is it always easy? Of course not. Do we experience more emotional roller coasters than we ever dreamed possible? Certainly. Did it push us out of our comfort zone? You bet it did. Did it change our lives? Yep, sure did. Has our faith grown and have we experienced God in ways we otherwise wouldn't have? Absolutely. Do I regret it? Nope, not even a little. I cannot even begin to describe to you all the ways God has used, and is still using, this opportunity to grow me and my husband. We are taking what God has given us and we are putting it to work. Please don't think I'm suggesting that I'm a ten-bags-of-gold-kinda-girl. God is still doing a work in me and I have a *very* long way to go before I am treating everything I have as a gift and deliberately seeking to multiply it. But I can tell you this. Settling for ordinary is not an option. I crave straight-up crazy.[1]

Are you beginning to see how viewing *everything* as a gift is an entire game changer? If we will begin to look at everything as it really is – a gift - and look for ways to bless others with it – won't it rock our worlds? And the world of those around us?

Let's camp on the physical realm of gifts a bit longer. Consider this. What about your physical body? (Some of you are probably already mad with me for just mentioning it!) How many of us really treat our physical bodies as a gift from God? We only get one you know. How are we caring for it? I fear that some of us take better care of our cars

---

[1] *I am not suggesting that opening your home is a wise choice for everyone. Use your God-given discernment people.*

than we do our own bodies. We may be diligent about the type of gas we pour into our car but we are willing to eat just about anything. We make sure we get our oil changed so our engines keep running smoothly but we would prefer to park our rear ends on the couch and watch endless episodes of our favorite show rather than exercise to keep our hearts strong. (I'm totally guilty of this so don't think I'm throwing stones here. I'm the biggest X-Files junkie you'll ever meet and I can't even begin to count the hours of my life I have successfully wasted watching some Mulder and Scully.) If you believe that God has given you a radical, straight-up crazy calling and destiny, then you have to leave room for the belief that He gifted you with the physical body capable of enduring the pressure required to live it out. It doesn't take an Einstein to discern that we will be less productive if we are unhealthy. We can't do all God has called us to do if we are chronically tired, unfit, or unmotivated to take care of ourselves. Let me encourage you to begin thinking about your physical body as a gift. If you *are* healthy, praise God for the gift of your health! Make the most of it. Get out there and multiply that bag of gold!

Let's consider another often overlooked gift. *Time.* Time is truly a gift from God. You are only on this planet for a short time. You were chosen by God to live in this generation. God chose and appointed you to be a light in the darkness of our current day. God gives all of us the time we need to do what He has called us to do. If you find yourself often overwhelmed, exhausted, and not able to catch up or keep up, then your plate is too full. God's serving size of responsibilities will never overflow off your plate. If overwhelmed or exhausted describes how you feel, pray for discernment to know what you need to take off your plate. Don't get the responsibilities of your radical destiny confused with the expectations or demands that others may have placed on you – including yourself.

Taking the challenge to start viewing everything as a gift is risky. If you view everything including your physical body, time, and all your possessions as a gift, you *will* start living differently – and by differently I mean you are going to look flat weird to everyone else around you because it's not the norm. You will probably encounter pressure from others who will encourage you to think about yourself more. However, when we grow in the mindset that everything we have is a gift from God and it's our responsibility to multiply it – it really will change everything.

FAN THE FLAME

As much as I'd like to pretend this parable didn't include the guy with just one bag of gold, I can't ignore him. Did you notice why he didn't do anything with his bag? He was afraid. Fear is a primary reason why Christians don't use the gifts they've **Fear** is the **greatest antithesis** of straight-up crazy. been given to their fullest potential. *Fear is the greatest antithesis of straight-up crazy.* Fear causes big buts. Fear keeps us in the boat. Fear cripples our ability to trust God. Fear hinders our obedience. Fear keeps us backed into a corner where we become mere spectators of others who are daring enough to multiple their bags of gold. The apostle Paul spotted this tendency in his young protégé, Timothy. Timothy was given the spiritual gift of preaching. Scholars agree that Timothy was probably a timid young man and that's why Paul reminded him that God had not given him a spirit of fear (2 Timothy 1:7). Paul encouraged Timothy to fan his gift into flame (2 Timothy 1:6). Picture a coal that has been kicked away from the fire. Its red hot glow rapidly diminishes. But what happens when you blow on it? It quickly regains its fiery glow. Unless you and I continuously and purposefully fan the flame of our gifts they will begin to fade and will go unused. How do we fan the flame? By *using* our gifts. We must deliberately put ourselves in situations that require us to use our gifts. For example, if your gift is teaching, but you fear speaking in front of people, you sign up to teach that class anyway. *Do it afraid. Fan the flame. Use your gift.* Remember that God has given you a spirit of power, love and self-discipline, so go for it! Multiply that bag of gold! Wanna know something cool? When you push past your fear and make every effort to start multiplying your bag of gold, you will start to enjoy it. That's right, *you will enjoy it!* Dare I say, it will make you happy! Did you catch what the master in the parable told the servants who had increased their bags? "Come and share in your master's happiness!" (vs.21, 23). There is something incredible about knowing when we push past our fear and use our gifts that we are making God *happy.* And that we get to share in His happiness! Now that's just straight-up crazy, isn't it?

> *We have different gifts, according to the grace given to each of us. If your gift is prophesying, then prophesy in accordance with your faith; if it is serving, then serve; if it is teaching then teach; if it is to encourage, then give encouragement; if it is giving, then give generously, if it is to lead, do it diligently; if it is to show mercy, do it cheerfully.*
> *Romans 12:6-8*

Since we're on the subject of gifts, I feel compelled to mention the risk of believing your radical calling and destiny is all about your gift. Once we start fanning the flame of our gift we can sometimes be tempted to get caught up in the enjoyment and attention that the gift may bring. This is a dangerous road to go down because this road can lead to worshipping the gift rather than the gift-giver. If we begin to feed on the attention and accolades that our gift brings us, we will lose sight of the reason God gave us the gift in the first place. Your calling is never about your gifts but rather your gifts are about your calling. I'm certainly not suggesting that enjoying your gift is wrong. Obviously from what we just read, using your gift lets you share in God's happiness! God *wants* you to delight in the gift He's given you. Who wants to give someone a gift and watch them begrudgingly use it? Of course you should enjoy your gift! But, your gift should never be the source of your joy. The ultimate source of your joy should always come from the giver of the gift.

This chapter certainly isn't an exhaustive overview about all gifts. However, there is one more type of gift that I do want to include. Personally, I think these gifts are more often overlooked than the ones previously mentioned. These gifts are the gifts that God has given us purely for our enjoyment. These gifts are everywhere but sadly go unnoticed often. Let me share a few with you that I experienced just today. *Yellow finches and hummingbirds. Red parasol flowers. A groundhog swimming in the pond behind my house. Coffee. Lots of coffee. Sweet kisses from my dog. A cool summer breeze. Dark chocolate. A highly energetic mocking bird. Wind chimes.* God's gifts to us for our pure enjoyment are all around us and when you and I take the time to thank Him for these gifts He smiles on us. I know that when I look for these gifts and delight in them my heart is lighter. Part of straight-up crazy is living in a constant state of awareness of the gifts all around us and in us: the gifts we've been given to accomplish and fulfill our destinies, the gifts we are responsible to multiply, and the sweet gifts our Father gives us for our pure delight. If you have ever been around someone whose living in a constant awareness of their gifts then my guess is you've been around someone who's straight-up crazy.

—PERSONAL STUDY QUESTIONS—

1. God's power and truth always trump our facts.

    a. Identify a current struggle or challenging situation in your life that seems impossible to conquer or solve. Write down some facts about this situation. What are the major challenges? Frustrations? Limitations? When you're finished, set your writing aside for a few minutes.

    b. Read Psalm 29. What are some words or phrases that describe God's power?

    c. Now read Genesis 1:1-10. As you read, try to form a picture in your mind of the events that are described. What would it look like for light to appear out of complete darkness? How much strength would it take to lift all of the rain water up above the sky, and to move the oceans and continents around on the Earth? What does this teach us about God? Could anything be impossible for the One who accomplished these things? Is there any need that He could not meet?

    d. Now go back to your writing. Considering what you've just read, write down some Truths about your situation.

2. Think about the boy who gave his lunch of fish and bread in the story told in Mark 6 and John 6.

    a. Do you think he thought it would be enough to feed thousands of people?

    b. Who benefitted from his choice to give his lunch?

    (Hint: there's more than one answer!)

    c. What do you think would have happened if he had chosen not to offer it?

3. Read the account of the Good Samaritan in Luke 10:25-37 and answer the following questions:

    a. What were the Good Samaritan's gifts? How did he choose to use them? How did it affect the man who had been injured? How do you think it would have affected the innkeeper?

    b. Consider and list some of the reasons why you think the priest didn't want to help. Have you ever identified with the priest? If so, how? What did you learn from the experience?

    c. Have you ever identified with the injured man in the parable? If so, how? If you experienced a "Good Samaritan," describe how it affected you.

    d. Jesus told the expert in the law to "Go and do likewise" (v.37). Who are your neighbors? What are some practical ways you can share your gifts with those around you?

4. Take a few minutes to write down some of the gifts that you've been given.

    Physical possessions...

    Spiritual gifts...

    Natural abilities...

    Situations...

    Relationships...

5. Write a prayer offering your gifts back to God. Ask Him to show you how He wants to use the gifts He has given you for the good of others, your own joy, and His glory. Ask Him for the courage to push past your fears and live straight-up crazy.

——————— COFFEE CHATS ———————

1. Talk about a situation you've seen or experienced in the past in which you saw God do the "impossible." What did this situation teach you about God's power and character?

2. Do you have a gift which you've been hesitant to place in the hands of Jesus? What is holding you back? Do you feel like it's not enough? What fears hold you back? What would it take for you to step out in straight-up crazy faith and trust God to apply His godly multiplication?

3. What have you been given? Chat about the different types of gifts God has given you.

4. In what ways is God calling you to push past your fears and doubts and to use your gifts?

Questions by Erika Scheck

CHAPTER EIGHT

NOT QUITE FINISHED JUST YET

With this in mind, we constantly pray for you, that our God may make you worthy of His calling, and that by His power He may bring to fruition your every desire for goodness and your every deed prompted by faith. We pray this so that the name of our Lord Jesus may be glorified in you, and you in Him. 2 Thessalonians 1:11-12

"He is no fool who gives what he cannot keep to gain what he cannot lose." Jim Elliot

"Nothing is better for our spiritual development than a big dream because it keeps us on our knees in raw dependence on God." Mark Batterson[1]

"If you want God to do something different in your life, you can't do the same old thing. It will involve more sacrifice, but if you are willing to go there, you'll realize you didn't sacrifice anything at all. It will involve more risk, but if you are willing to go there, you'll realize you didn't risk anything at all." Mark Batterson[2]

PASSIONS • DESIRES
DREAMS • DESTINIES

Can I talk you into having one last cup of coffee with me before I wrap

this thing up? I realize I've already said a lot, but I'm not quite finished

just yet. There is one final topic I want us to talk about before we call it

> If you make the Destiny-Giver
> your goal, then you will
> **discover your destiny.**

a day. I think it's a pretty big deal. I happen to believe it's the defining

factor between you just being normal or being straight-up crazy. It

most definitely will require radical faith. It will also demand a massive

amount of trust and far-reaching obedience. It will require fierce per-

severance and an unyielding determination to never quit or give up.

You certainly won't be able to do it from inside your boat and there's

not a snowball's chance in Arizona of you doing it if you have a big but.

You'll have to fight the enemy if you pursue it because he undoubtedly

won't like it. He will work exceedingly hard to discourage and distract

you and he will do whatever he can to try and destroy you. He will do his very best to convince you that you are too weak and insignificant to do it and that your God is too small to handle it.

Are you wondering what kind of coffee conversation this is going to be? We're talking about God-given, God-sized passions and dreams that lead to radical destinies. I'm not sure where I first heard the phrase "God-sized dream," but I *do* remember sitting in church one Sunday and hearing something that has stuck with me for more than a decade now. I couldn't tell you what the sermon as a whole was about that morning but my pastor articulated one powerful phrase that struck a chord deep inside of me. This singular phrase was the catalyst that transformed the entire trajectory of my life. He said,

> "Pray for a **passion** that will give you a **vision** that will lead to a story."[1]

The pages of your destiny will tell your story. Never forget that your destiny is rooted in your call to *go,* but that's not all it is; it's much, much more. You were born on purpose with a purpose. Your destiny is as unique as your fingerprint. When you pursue a God-sized dream, you are pursuing your radical destiny. A God-sized dream always be-

---

[1] *April 2009, sermon by Dr. Gary Johnson. The only reason I remember the date is because I wrote it in my Bible. I knew when I heard it that my life was about to change.*

gins with a passion, but not just any passion, a *God-given* passion. A God-given passion and a God-sized dream go hand in hand. Where

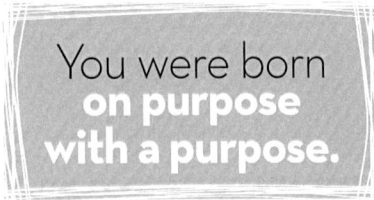

> You were born **on purpose with a purpose.**

you find one - you will find the other. Like peanut butter and jelly. Starsky and Hutch. Yin and yang. Sonny and Cher, well, maybe not. You get the point.[1] Let me clarify what I'm talking about when I say passion. There are lots of people who are passionate about lots of things but that doesn't mean they are all God-given passions. I'll be the first to admit that I'm an over-the-top-a-little-too-crazy-passionate about Kentucky basketball. (Go Cats!) In my humble opinion, UK is the only college basketball team worthy of passion, but that's not the kind of passion I'm talking about.[2] I'm talking about passion that can *change the world*. A God-given passion is a passion that will cause your heart to beat in rhythm with the heartbeat of God. His heart *always* beats in rhythm with His perfect will. If we are going to be able to discern God's will, we must know what He is passionate about, namely: *what delights the heart of God, what breaks the heart of God and what moves the heart of God*. When your heartbeat is in rhythm with God's heartbeat, you will find yourself living out your radical destiny and changing the world.

---

[1] *Mulder and Scully. Popcorn and Coke®. Oreos® and milk. I could do this all day long.*
[2] *If you aren't a fellow UK fan then that's okay, we can still be friends. Unless you are a Duke fan. Then probably not.*

> A God-given passion is a passion that will cause **your heart** to beat in rhythm with the **heartbeat of God.** His heart always beats in rhythm with His perfect will.

Let's go back to the beginning. Not the beginning of this book; the very beginning of all time. We discover so much about the God of Creation in the first three chapters of Genesis, including what *delights*, *breaks* and *moves* His heart. Our God is not a God that hides Himself choosing to remain mysterious and unknown. Instead, He has made Himself known to His creation since the commencement of time. God never hides or teases us by saying, "Find me if you can!" He never disguises His motives or masks His desires. Not only is He the God who sees, hears, knows and rescues, He is also the God who *wants* to be seen, heard, known and experienced as our Rescuer. God is not like a puzzle that we have to try and put together. He has put Himself on display so anyone who wants to know Him, can.

—— IN THE BEGINNING... ——

At creation, God put on the most amazing show that had ever been. First He spoke the world into existence, then He created all the plants, animals, birds and fish. All of this was a great crescendo leading up to the most spectacular grand finale of all time – the creation of Adam and Eve. When He was finished with His creation show, He stepped back, took a deep holy breath, rested and *delighted* in His creation, "God saw all that He had made, and it was *very* good" (Genesis 1:31, my emphasis). As awesome as all of creation was (especially the dogs, horses, birds and Caribbean water, obviously) God especially delighted in Adam and Eve. They were the crowning glory of all He had created because they were created in His image. They shared a unique, intimate and personal relationship with their Creator. Sadly, it didn't take long for this perfection to be tarnished by sin. When Adam and Eve chose to sin against God, His heart was *broken* because their perfect relationship was disrupted and marred. Thankfully, God's heart was also *moved* by their need to be forgiven, rescued and restored. He covered their sin by covering them with garments of animal skin – this being the very first blood sacrifice. Isn't God's Word amazing? Right there in the very beginning of the very first book in the Bible, in the very beginning of time, thousands of years before Jesus came to earth, is a picture of Christ's atoning work on the cross to cover our sin and make a way for us to be in a relationship with God.

God doesn't change. God's heart is the same today as it was then. He delights in His creation. His heart breaks over the separation sin causes. His

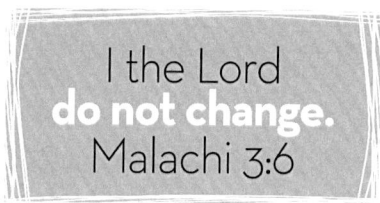

> I the Lord **do not change.** Malachi 3:6

heart always moves to rescue those who are lost. I believe there is a verse that beautifully paints the full picture of the heartbeat of God:

> *For God so loved the world that He gave His one and only*
> *Son that whoever believes in Him shall not perish but have*
> *eternal life. John 3:16*

So what does all of this have to do with God-sized passions and dreams? When you and I meditate on, delight in and fully embrace the timeless truth of what delights, breaks and moves the heart of God, our hearts begin to beat in tune with His heartbeat. Then something straight-up amazing happens…

> *Take delight in the Lord and He will give you the desires of*
> *your heart. Psalm 37:4*

—DELIGHT, DESIRE AND PASSION—

In John 15, Jesus talks about God the Father as the gardener. Imagine Him walking through His garden, diligently searching for hearts that delight in Him and in His unshakable and unchanging truths. Those hearts, the ones who take pure delight in Him, are the ones that He leans over and lovingly plants the seeds of His desires in their fertile soil. If carefully nurtured and watered, those seeds will grow into strong desires and burning passions that reflect His desires and passions. Your heart will delight in the same things that your Father delights in. Your heart will break over the same things that break His heart. And your heart will be moved by the same things that move His heart. This is the transforming work of the Holy Spirit making you and me more and more like Jesus. The strongest and most passionate hearts are those that beat in rhythm with the heartbeat of God.

"You are unique. Just like everyone else."

This was a quote on a poster I saw a while back. It was meant to be sarcastically funny, but there is actually a lot of truth to it when you think about it. You *are* unique. We all are. When God knit you together in your mother's womb, He gave you distinct fingerprints that are unlike any other's on the planet. Not to mention no one thinks like you do or dreams like you do. No one else has your personality. You were fearfully and wonderfully made (Psalm 139:14). God created you to do what only you can do. He is the gardener who will plant His desires, passions and dreams in your heart uniquely suited and carefully planned out just for you.

You are meant to have a radical destiny. Your life is meant to mean something. You are meant to leave a mark on the timeline of history. Your destiny is unique to you. No one can live your destiny like you can. Remember the time we spent talking about Ephesians 2:10? "For we are God's handiwork, created in Christ Jesus to do good works, which God prepared in advance for us to do." Your destiny includes good works that God planned for *you* before the beginning of time! That means even before God opened His mouth and spoke the universe into existence, before the sun rose and set marking the very first day, before He walked with Adam and Eve in the garden, He already had in mind what He wanted you to do. *You were created on purpose for a purpose.* You discover your purpose when your heart beats in rhythm with the heartbeat of God.

You won't find anyone more fervent and driven by their passion than Jesus Himself. His heart *literally* beat in rhythm with the heartbeat of God. Think about it. His passion and desire was and is to love and to rescue. This unbridled desire compelled Him to lay aside His rightful place in Heaven and follow His passion…

> *Christ Jesus, who, being in very nature God, did not consider equality with God something to be used to His own advantage; rather He made Himself nothing by taking the very nature of a servant, being made in human likeness. And being found in appearance as a man, He humbled Himself by becoming obedient to death – even death on a cross! Philippians 2:6-8*

Pray for a **passion** that will lead to a **vision...**

Jesus' heartbeat was in perfect rhythm with His Father's heartbeat. His passion was to rescue you and me from our sin and restore our relationship with Him. From the time that Jesus took His first breath as a man, His vision and His purpose was to rescue and the only means by which this was possible was by the way of the cross. Allow me to camp here for a minute because I think we need to spend some time thinking through the implications of what I just asserted. Just to be clear, I'm saying that *Jesus Christ was driven by His passion to save us and it was His radical destiny to die on the cross.* His passion and vision were the direct outpouring of the heartbeat of God. His passion led to great triumph and victory but it also came with a great deal of pain and suffering. Why do I want to camp here? Because I fear too frequently in our overly comfortable, make-it-all-about-me Christian culture, we are often told that the primary purpose or goal of a God-sized dream and passion is to make much of us. Happy. Popular. Admired. Comfortable. The meaning of the verse in Psalm 37:4 has been twisted to say that if we delight in the Lord, He will give us the desires of *our* heart. I remember wrestling with this verse before I came to understand its true meaning. I thought, "I need to figure out what delighting in the Lord means so He will give me what I want." When we interpret this verse from our own selfish viewpoint, it sounds like a magical formula we can use to get God to give us whatever our hearts want: a bigger house, a nicer car, a better job, a perfect spouse, the perfect number of children, the right amount of money in our bank account and maybe even a gazillion followers on Twitter. I'm not saying God *won't* do those things but I am saying that it's certainly

Jesus Christ was driven by His passion **to save us** and it was His radical destiny to **die on the cross.**

not His priority. God isn't concerned with our happiness per se; He is concerned about our holiness and our hearts beating in tune with His. He certainly isn't concerned with how many followers we have on social media; instead He's concerned with how many followers He has! God's heart beats for the lost to know Him, for the hopeless to know hope, for the orphans to have families, for the broken to find healing and wholeness, and for us to know and experience pure joy and delight through an intimate relationship with Him. Here's the for-real deal about God-sized dreams and passions: *The pursuit of our God-sized dreams won't always feel good.* It won't always be easy. The truth of the matter is sometimes it's just down right hard. There will be times when we will question if we are on the right road. We may wonder why in the world we signed up for straight-up crazy. There will be times when others will watch us make sacrifices and they will think we have lost our minds, leaving us feeling vulnerable and very alone. But the truth is, no matter what the cost, *Jesus is worth it.* We will never pursue our God-sized dreams in vain.

When God plants His desires in our hearts, they grow into God-sized passions and dreams that will bring glory to Jesus. *It's all about Jesus.* There was nothing glamorous about Jesus leaving the splendor and perfection of Heaven to come to earth as a servant and to ultimately give His life as a ransom for you and for me. *His passion led Him to suffer and to make the ultimate sacrifice.* Be aware that your passion will lead you down a road where you will face suffering and sacrifice will be required. If there isn't suffering to some degree and you have not had to make any sacrifices associated with your God-sized dream and passion, then you may want to reassess your dream. Is it indeed a passion that God planted in your heart or is it simply your own desire? *"Everyone who wants to live a godly life in Christ Jesus will be persecuted"* (2 Timothy 3:12). Despite the hardship and suffering, there is tremendous joy in the pursuit of a God-sized dream and a beautiful irony in God-given passions. Jesus told us plainly…

> *Whoever wants to be my disciple must deny themselves and take up their cross daily and follow me. For whoever wants to save their life will lose it, but whoever loses their life for me will save it. Luke 9:23-24*

When we make the decision to rid our hearts of our selfish desires (denying ourselves) and invite God to plant His desires in our hearts, our heartbeat will match His. When our heartbeat is in rhythm with God's heartbeat, our passions and desires unlock the door of the abundant life Jesus promised. Don't be deceived by the enemy. He will try and convince you that by dying to your own desires and passions you will be dying to all that is worth living for. Jesus said that the enemy comes to steal, kill and destroy. Jesus came that we might have abundant life (John 10:10). Abundant life is full of godly passion and godly desires. It's made up of God-sized dreams where you get to experience Him doing the impossible in you and through you. Dying to yourself is the beginning of truly living. God-given passions and dreams will guide our footsteps on the road to our destiny. *We will find our life when we lose it.*

> We will **find** our life when we **lose** it.

I've talked a lot about some of my favorite people in the Bible: Moses, Peter, and Jehoshaphat. But what kind of weirdo would I be if I didn't talk about Paul in a book about straight-up crazy and radical faith? If any dude in Scripture displayed radical faith and lived straight-up crazy, it was definitely Paul. I don't believe that anyone who ever came in contact with Paul could accuse him of being tepid, mediocre or complacent. Paul was definitely on-fire and filled with Godly passion for sure.

One would only need to do a cursory reading of the letters written by Paul in the New Testament to determine what he was passionate about. Paul was over-the-top passionate about spreading the gospel of Jesus Christ. This guy knew *from experience* the transforming power of Jesus and he wanted everyone else to experience it too.[1] He says in 1 Corinthians 9:16, "I am compelled to preach. Woe to me if I do not preach the gospel!" The KJV renders this verse, "For though I preach the gospel, I have nothing to glory of; for necessity is laid upon me; yea, woe is unto me, if I preach not the gospel!" The word "necessity" means "necessity, imposed either by the circumstances, or by law of duty regarding to one's advantage."[2] Paul preached the gospel of Jesus Christ out of sheer necessity. It was what he *had* to do even though he knew that his passion would lead him straight down a road marked with suffering:

> And now, compelled by the Spirit, I am going to Jerusalem, not knowing what will happen to me there. I only know that in every city the Holy Spirit warns me that prison and hardships are facing me. However, I consider my life worth nothing to me, if only I may finish the race and complete the task the Lord Jesus has given me – the task of testifying to the gospel of God's grace. Acts 20:22-24

This passage gets to me every time I read it! Man, I want to be as passionate as Paul! He knew hardships and suffering were part of

---

[1] If you aren't familiar with Paul's radical transformation, I strongly encourage you to read what happened in Paul's own words in Acts 22:2-21.
[2] Strong's Concordance

the God-sized dream package but He believed Jesus was worth it all. Paul's God-sized dream was to testify to the gospel of God's grace to as many as would listen. God-sized dreams and passions will *compel* us to go where it's not comfortable. Paul used the Greek word "deō" for "compel" and it means "to tie, to bind, to imprison, to throw into chains."[1] This paints a pretty serious picture of how Paul viewed his relationship with the Holy Spirit. Sounds to me like Paul was so deeply connected to, bound to, *chained to* the Holy Spirit of God that if he were to do something other than what God was compelling him to do, his heart might just quit beating. When our heartbeats match the rhythm of God's heartbeat, we will be compelled to do what doesn't come to us naturally. We will consider others before ourselves, kiss our comfort zone goodbye and get out of the dang boat. We will look pain and suffering in the face and not retreat in fear. Were you perhaps wondering about the phrase "I consider my life worth nothing to me"? This wasn't a self-pity statement or depression talking. Paul understood that the Lord Jesus Christ counted his life as worth dying for, therefore, Paul could willingly lay down his life knowing Jesus would raise it up. Paul was passionate about what God was passionate about and his heart beat in tune with the heartbeat of God. Paul found his life when he lost it, and it's when we will find ours too.

[1] *Strong's Concordance*

I realize that there is a chance that you may be reading this and thinking that you have no idea what your God-sized dreams are. Maybe as you were growing up you dreamed about being a famous actor and you liked to imagine how awesome it would be to play the character that everyone loved to hate on a daytime soap opera.[1] Not only did reality set in but you also realized this wasn't exactly the plan God had for you. So how do you begin to discover your God-sized dream? First, you must *believe* that God will in fact plant His desires and passions in your heart...*if you ask Him to.* This is one area where you don't want to be guilty of not having because you didn't ask (James 4:2). Let me point you back to what my pastor said, "Pray for a passion that will lead to a vision that will give you a story." Pray fervently, consistently, and desperately for God to plant His desires in your heart. Then start paying close attention to what moves you. You will most likely have to make some changes in your life. If you have never noticed what moves you it may be because you have allowed your heart to be numbed by other things that don't require passion. Sometimes we allow things to numb our hearts so we won't have to feel. Things such as excessive amounts of television, obsession with social media, continuous communication that never goes below the surface level, constant busyness and all different types of addictions. We are easily distracted and can be prevented from seeing the world the way

[3]*Obviously I'm talking about someone I knew in High School. And by someone I obviously mean me.*

God sees it and feeling how He feels about it. But when we tune our hearts to His, we *will* see and feel differently. Hearts in rhythm with His are hearts of fertile soil where God's passions and desires can grow.

> *You will never lighten any load until you feel the pressure in your own soul. –Ravi Zacharias[1]*

After Paul's conversion, he began to see everything and everyone differently. He did a complete 180^0 turn-around. Leaving everything he'd ever known behind, he moved forward in trust and obedience and pursued His God-given passion with everything he had in him. Do you fear what God may call you to give up or leave behind if you pray for His desires in your heart? Paul had something to say about what he once had and how he gave it up…

> *Whatever were gains to me I now consider loss for the sake of Christ. What is more, I consider everything a loss because of the surpassing worth of knowing Christ Jesus my Lord, for whose sake I have lost all things. I consider them garbage, that I may gain Christ and be found in Him, not having a righteousness that comes from the law, but that which is through faith in Christ – the righteousness that comes from God on the basis of faith. Philippians 2:7-9*

[1] Ravi Zacharias (@RaviZacharias) 5.17.14 Tweet

When you begin to feel passionate about something, your God-sized dream will begin to take shape. Pursue it. Chase it. Settle for nothing less. Refuse to remain comfortable. Fight mediocrity. Be strong and courageous. Know that your God is with you. You were born for passion and purpose. God has a dream just for you. Your God-sized dreams will help change the world.

Don't be afraid of what God may ask you to give up. Instead, be afraid of missing out on God doing the impossible through you if you don't chase your passion. You don't really want to come to the end of your life and think, "Whew! Glad I played it safe!" do you? Nothing makes me more nauseous than thinking about laying on my deathbed and knowing I didn't pursue straight-up crazy because I was too afraid or didn't want to be uncomfortable. God help me. *God help all of us.* Wouldn't we much rather give it all we've got? I'm willing to look straight-up crazy - what about you? Are we willing to take risks? Are we willing to fail? When we believe that there is no greater failure than failing to trust God, we will be willing to fall, knowing He will be faithful to pick us back up.

When I first started on this straight-up crazy journey of mine, God planted His passions and desires in my heart. First, He gave me an insatiable hunger for His Word. His Word brought me life and freedom I had never known before. Soon it wasn't enough for me just to personally study and enjoy His Word. I resonated deeply with the words of Jeremiah the prophet, "His Word is in my heart like a fire, a fire shut up in my bones. I am weary of holding it in; indeed, I cannot" (Jeremiah 20:9). It's not enough for me to study God's Word – I am *compelled* to teach it!

My desire to do what God was calling me to do outweighed my own heart's desire to play it safe. *Hello, I was born painfully shy!* It was extremely difficult for me to get up in front of anyone and speak my name, let alone teach God's Word! I am living proof that God is faithful to give us what we need to do what He has called us to do. It didn't happen overnight, but little by little God began to grow in me a great confidence. Hear me clearly: this new found confidence is in *His* ability, not my own! The more I was obedient, the more I got to experience His faithfulness. Here's what I've learned about God-sized dreams and passions – they cannot be contained. There's no tapping out. They continue to grow and grow even when you think your dreams have reached the sky's limit, God gives you even more passion and bigger and crazier dreams.

God gave me the desire to teach His Word. Now, I not only want to teach my sweet little Bible study group at my home church – *I want to teach the masses.* But that's not all. I want to build a platform for other Bible study teachers to teach the masses. I desire for every woman in the nation and eventually – *the world* – to have access to relevant and in-depth Bible studies because I know from *experience* that God's Word changes people and sets us free! I dream of a unified community of women from every race, background, and denomination coming together to love and serve each other and grow in their love for God. I imagine countless women connecting across the globe with other women who share similar life experiences to encourage and comfort one another. I dream of partnering with large Not-For-Profit agencies who work hard to change the world by abolishing human slavery, ending abortion, eradicating poverty and feeding the hungry, and empowering them to do even more. And I have many more straight-up crazy dreams and passions. Heck, I'm just getting started! I can't do it on my own. It's too big and too hard for me, but it's not too big or too hard for God. He has been faithful to give me what I need to do what He has called me to do.

What about you? What delights your heart? Is it working with children? Assisting the elderly? Teaching God's Word? Think about what breaks your heart. Is it the human trafficking crisis? Or thinking about people groups that haven't yet heard the gospel? Maybe your heart breaks when you think of children who are orphans that need a family. What moves your heart? Foreign missions? The plight of single moms, or the great need for healthy foster care families? Do you have a passion to love on and reach the homosexual community and show them the love of Jesus? Maybe your heart is moved when you think about counseling the depressed, broken and those filled with despair and their need to hear about hope in Jesus. The list could go on and on. *If you are a follower of Christ, He WILL plant His passions in your heart. He WILL give you a dream.* Remember, you were born on purpose with a purpose. The question is, will you pursue it? Will you make the decision to believe God, kick your faith up to a radical notch and be willing to pursue *straight-up crazy?* This dark world needs followers of Jesus whose hearts beat in rhythm with His. Your God-sized dream could change the world.

EPILOGUE

RUn THe RACe
FIGHT THe gOOD FIGHT
GeT THe PRIZE

There's not a single example in the entire Word of God that would lead us to believe we could believe God in vain. We are told over and over again that if we persevere, if we labor, if we never, ever, ever give up, we *will* reap a harvest. God will bring to fruition our every desire for goodness and every deed prompted by our faith (2 Thessalonians 1:11).

As we near the bottom of our coffee cups, I want to leave you with an encouraging truth that God reminded me of this morning. I was reading the parable of the sower in Luke 8:4-15. Listen with fresh ears what Jesus said in verse 15:

But the seed on good soil stands for those with a noble and good heart, who hear the word, retain it, and by persevering produce a crop.

We are beyond blessed to have the Word of God at our fingertips. We can hear it and read it any time we like and at our leisure and convenience. The question we have to ask ourselves is, are we retaining it? Are we persevering? Because if we can answer yes to those questions, Jesus said we *will* produce a crop.

The key for us is to persevere. Paul refers to this journey as a race. Living a life that is marked by radical faith and straight-up crazy will require perseverance. An unyielding, steadfast and a determined will to never, ever give up. Paul was determined to "finish the race and complete the task" that Jesus had given him (Acts 20:24). We are running a marathon, not a sprint.

> *Do you not know that in a race all the runners run, but only*
> *one gets the prize? Run in such a way as to get the prize.*
> *1 Corinthians 9:24*

Running the race to gain the prize requires perseverance. The reward? A harvest. A realized God-sized dream. A lifetime of straight-up crazy. The fruit of radical faith.

> *Let us not become weary in doing good, for at the*
> *proper time we will reap a harvest if we don't give up.*
> *Galatians 6:9*

Paul knew running the race meant a lifetime commitment. He was in it for the long haul. His dream of preaching the gospel to the nations was a dream that would carry him through to the end of his life. Listen to how he described it to the believers in Philippi:

> I'm not saying that I have all this together, that I have it made. But I'm well on my way, reaching out for Christ, who has so wondrously reached out for me. Friends, don't get me wrong: By no means do I count myself as an expert in all of this, but I've got my eye on the goal, where God is beckoning us onward – to Jesus. I'm off and running, and I'm not turning back. *Philippians 3:12-14, MSG*

Don't you love it? "I'm off and running and I'm not turning back."

Early on I posed a lot of "What If?" questions. What if your destiny had eternal significance? What would our world look like if you were convinced God would do the impossible in you and through you? What if you truly understood that your radical destiny is rooted in your calling to go?

I'm asking God to give you – *yes, you* – the gift of radical faith. I'm asking God to give you a heart that believes your destiny has eternal significance and that He absolutely can and will do the impossible in you and through you. I believe He will give you a straight-up crazy dream that can and will change the world. I believe that if you make Jesus Christ your goal you will run the race God has marked out just for you, and that you will run it well. Never quitting, never giving up, no matter the cost. *Because Jesus is worth it.*

Let's do this. Let's chase straight-up crazy together during the time that God has given us on this planet. Let's make waves in our generation that will affect the generations to come. Let's make our lives count. Let's encourage one another to get out of the boat. Let's fight the enemy together side by side. Let's run this race for the prize, expect a harvest and finish well.

Straight-up crazy 'til the very end.

> *I have fought the good fight, I have finished the race, I have kept the faith. 2 Timothy 4:7*

—PERSONAL STUDY QUESTIONS—

1. Read 2 Corinthians 11:22 – 12:10 and answer the following questions.

   a. After all the hardships and sufferings Paul endured, how do you think he was able to say, "I delight in weaknesses, in insults, in hardships, in persecutions, in difficulties" (2 Cor. 12:10)?

   b. Can you personally relate to Paul's prayer asking God to relieve him of his "thorn in the flesh" (2 Cor. 12:7-8)? If so, how? How has your faith grown as a result? Describe how your "thorn" has helped you relate to others who also suffer.

   c. Are you able to say with Paul, "When I am weak, then I am strong" (2 Cor. 12:10)?

2. Read the following passages: Acts 4:1-4, Acts 7:54 – 8:4, Philippians 1:12-14.

   Answer the following questions:

   a. What do these passages have in common?

   b. How do these verses relate to what Jesus said in Matthew 5:10-12?

    c. How did the perseverance of these first century followers of Jesus work to advance the gospel?

    d. Explain how your most difficult times could increase the advancement of God's kingdom.

3. Read Ephesians 2:10. Have you discovered some of the "good works" that God prepared in advance for you to do? What are they? Do you believe that you are actively seeking to accomplish God's desires for your life? What changes do you need to make in order for you to recognize God's dream for you?

4. Read Joshua 6 and consider the following questions.

    a. How would Joshua and the Israelites have viewed the wall of Jericho?

    b. Would God's instructions have made logical sense to them?

    c. Why do you suppose they chose to be obedient?

    d. Inhabiting this land was a dream that God had planted in their hearts long before this day. Was this a dream that they could accomplish on their own? What was their responsibility in realizing the dream? What was God's responsibility?

5. Write a prayer expressing your desire to remain faithful during times of suffering. Sincerely ask God to plant His desires in your heart, giving you a God-sized dream. Ask that He will give you the strength and courage needed to work toward those dreams. And pray for radical faith to believe He will do the impossible in you and through you! Pray that you will settle for nothing less than straight-up crazy.

───── COFFEE CHATS ─────

1. Is it difficult for you to talk about your God-sized dream out loud? Why or why not? What could a benefit be from talking about it with others?

2. If money and resources were not an obstacle, what is one thing you would love to do?

3. How have your dreams been shaped by your circumstances and life experiences?

4. What scares you the most about not pursuing a God-sized dream?

5. What are you most passionate about?

6. How are you pursuing your God-sized dream? How is it "too big" for you? In what ways do you need God to intervene?

QUOTE REFERENCES

Chapter One
1Christine Caine (@ChristineCaine) 7.31.14 Tweet
2Susie Larson, *Your Beautiful Purpose: Discovering and Enjoying What God Can Do Through You* (Bloomington, Minnesota: Bethany House Publishing, 2013), 19.

Chapter Two
1James MacDonald (@jamesmacdonald) 6.22.14 Tweet

Chapter Three
1David Platt, *Radical: Taking Back Your Faith From the American Dream* (Colorado Springs, Colorado: Multonmah Books, 2010), 160.

Chapter Four
1Oswald Chambers. http://www.goodreads.com/author/quotes/41469.Oswald_Chambers
2A.W. Tozer. https://www.goodreads.com/author/quotes/1082290.A_W_Tozer

Chapter Five
1Jim Cymbala (@jimcymbala) 7.31.14 Tweet

Chapter Six
1Christine Caine (@ChristineCaine) 7.24.14 Tweet

Chapter Seven
1Mark Batterson, *The Circle Maker: Praying Circles Around Your Biggest Dreams and Greatest Fears* (Grand Rapids, Michigan: Zondervan, 2011), 30.

Chapter Eight
1Mark Batterson, *The Circle Maker: Praying Circles Around Your Biggest Dreams and Greatest Fears* (Grand Rapids, Michigan: Zondervan, 2011), 45.
2 Mark Batterson, *The Circle Maker: Praying Circles Around Your Biggest Dreams and Greatest Fears* (Grand Rapids, Michigan: Zondervan, 2011), 36.

ABOUT THE AUTHOR

PAULETTE STAMPER

Paulette has an unwavering desire and dedication to equip and empower as many followers of Christ as possible so they can live out a radical faith. Paulette's God-sized dream is for believers everywhere to discover their God-given purpose and live out their God-given destiny resulting in a movement that will change the world. She loves Jesus and is passionate about studying and teaching God's Word. She has authored two Bible studies (*Sand Surfers* and *Rescued*) and *Straight-Up Crazy* is her first book. She is the founder of Ignite Women, serves as a counselor at a local Christ-centered community center, and leads the local Ignite group at her home church. Paulette loves her husband and family and the awesome people in her life (including the cute but obnoxious furry white dog that rules her house). She loves a good commentary and eagerly consumes at least three good cups of coffee a day.

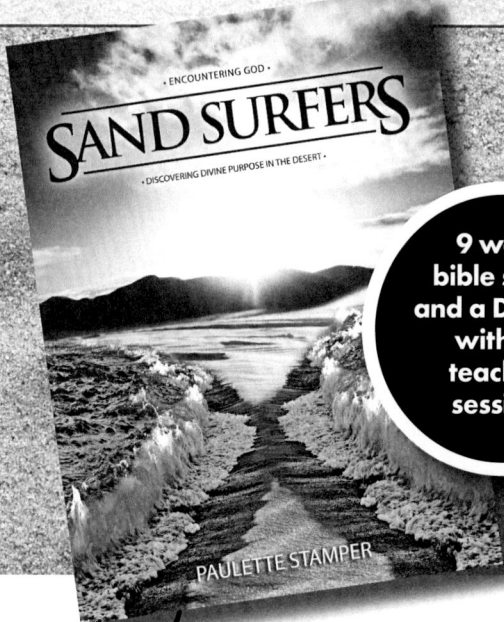

Rescued

a journey from darkness to light

Rescued, A Journey from Darkness to Light is a unique 6-week bible study based on the Apostle Paul's letter to the Colossians. In it, you will discover exciting and life-changing truths about who God is and who He says you are. You will "meet" several women who openly share their own journey of God's intimate work in their lives. Their stories will encourage and inspire you as you see God's word come to life through their personal experiences. As you embark on this journey, you too will experience God's personal movement in your life. He delights in rescuing those He loves, and He loves you! **Isn't it time for you to begin your journey from darkness to light?**